# NIGERIAN CIVIL WAR, 1967-70;

# AN ANNOTATED BIBLIOGRAPHY

by

Christian Chukwunedu Aguolu

G. K. HALL & CO., 70 LINCOLN STREET, BOSTON, MASS.
1973

**Library of Congress Cataloging in Publication Data**

Aguolu, Christian Chukwunedu, 1940-
   Nigerian Civil War, 1967-1970.

   1.  Nigeria--History--Civil War, 1967-1970--
Bibliography.  I.  Title.
Z3597.A642        016.9669'05          73-17123
ISBN 0-8161-1074-3

*This publication is printed on permanent/durable acid-free paper.*

ISBN 0-8161-1074-3

Dedicated to all those
who lost their lives
in the war.

# TABLE of CONTENTS

## Table of Contents

# INTRODUCTION

Nigeria, a former British colony, with a population of over sixty million is the most populous African nation. Blessed with plentiful natural resources, it is one of the world's largest producers of cocoa and petroleum.

Like other African countries marked by a high degree of ethnic divergence, Nigeria is plagued by tribalism - an inordinate, philosophical, emotional and intellectual attachment of its peoples to their ethnic groups. There are over 250 tribes with equal number of languages and dialects, differing also in culture, religion and philosophical outlook. The three major competing ethnic groups among these have engaged themselves for many decades in the struggle for political power and national dominance. In the North are the Moslem Hausa-Fulani; in the West the Yorubas, Christian, Moslem and animist; and in the East the Ibos, mostly receptive to Christianity. Until the overthrow of the civilian regime in January 15, 1966, the political structure was deeply grounded in ethnic and regional loyalties. With very powerful regional governments, the Federal Government had only a very precarious existence. Since 1960, when Nigeria gained its independence from Great Britain, there had been numerous crises which nearly brought the country to political disintegration. National censuses and political elections were very badly conducted and the politicians were avaricious and unscrupulous. Minority tribes perpetually, but ineffectually, demanded some degree of local autonomy from the indifferent majority ruling tribes.

However, much of the political unrest in Africa today is a colonial legacy. Colonial boundaries were artificially created to suit the interests of the European colonial bureaucracy with no relevance to African needs. The boundaries and governmental administrative jurisdictions in Africa were generally haphazard, and rather than narrowing the existing cultural gap, widened it. The transplants of British and French constitutional systems were imposed on Africans without any considerations for the unique differences between Africa and Europe. Nigeria, like other African nations, after gaining its independence was faced with the urgent task of devising a new constitutional system that was relevant to its needs and acceptable to its disparate tribal units. In such a multi-plural society as Nigeria where ethnic loyalty is strong, it has been difficult to devise a constitution acceptable to all. Professor Donald Rothchild, author of Toward unity in Africa: a study of federalism in British Africa (1960), has observed "Africa is faced with a situation of little flexibility regarding constitutional systems. It continues to need a formula that will reconcile the requirements of central leadership with the demands of regional autonomy."[1]

---

1. Donald S. Rothchild. "The Limits of federalism: an examination of political institutional transfer in Africa," J. Mod. Afr. Stud., IV (Nov. 1966), p. 292.

# Introduction

Although African leaders realize that colonial boundaries have constituted a serious source of political unrest for their nations, there seems to be a general feeling to leave the boundaries as they are. "The strong pressures to change them so as to give greater autonomy to dissatisfied national, racial, or religious groups are matched by widespread anxiety among African leaders to preserve national units big enough to avoid a dread 'Balkanization' or a reversion to tribalism."[2]

The period 1960-1966 in Nigeria was marked by bribery, nepotism, and brazen political patronage. On January 15, 1966, dissatisfied army elements, largely Ibo, in the Federal army - perhaps in an effort to stop the deliberate killings of political opponents in Western Nigeria during the political elections and revamp the Nigerian political system - toppled the Nigerian Federal Government, killing several national leaders. The political leadership of the country, thrust upon the Ibo Major-General Aguiyi-Ironsi, Supreme Commander of the Armed Forces, on January 16, ended on July 29, 1966, in another military coup led by Northern military elements in the Federal Army. General Ironsi and several Eastern Nigerian officers were killed. The political situation was deteriorating. On August 1, 1966, General Gowon (then a Lieutenant-Colonel) who, as a Christian from a minority tribe in Northern Nigeria and considered a moderate, assumed the leadership of the country in an attempt to prevent its break-up. Tribal antagonisms flared up in the North, and there was large-scale rioting resulting in the deaths of thousands of Easterners, mostly Ibo. Consequently, most Easterners in different parts of the country fled back to their homeland in the East. The All-Nigeria Ad Hoc Constitutional Conference held in Lagos in September 1966, to arrest the deteriorating situation was fruitless. The decisions of the historic meeting attended by all the Nigerian military leaders at Aburi, Ghana, on January 4-5, 1967, were differently interpreted by both the Federal and Eastern Nigerian authorities. The nature of the constitutional system to be adopted for Nigeria, the rioting in Northern Nigeria, and the refugee problems in the East had all been discussed at Aburi. The Eastern Nigerian Government accused the Federal Government of not honoring the decisions taken in Ghana, and the Federal Government contended otherwise. There were claims and counterclaims.

On May 30, 1967, Eastern Nigeria decided to go its own way and declared itself to be the "Independent Republic of Biafra." The Federal Government declared war on the secessionist state on July 6, 1967, in order to preserve its political unity and territorial integrity. The Great Powers took sides. Great Britain and the Soviet Union supported the Federal effort to crush the secession; France sympathized with the Biafrans; the United States claimed a political and military neutrality. The war, fought relentlessly for thirty months, took over two and a half million lives, mostly through starvation. On January 12, 1970, the secessionist forces capitulated to the Federal troops, and on January 15, the Republic of Biafra officially signed papers of surrender and ceased to exist, dissolving into the East Central, Rivers and South-East States in accordance with

---

2. London <u>Observer</u>, Jan. 1970.

# Introduction

the Federal Decree of May 27, 1967, which had divided the country into twelve states. However, the South-East and Rivers States, long captured from Biafra, had been under the Federal jurisdiction.

Nigeria's territorial integrity was then preserved. Since the end of the war, there has been a remarkable degree of national reconciliation and integration; the general economic recovery, especially in the East Central State, has gone beyond the expectations of even the optimists. There is reason to believe that before the Federal Military Government hands over power to a democratically constituted civilian government in 1976, (the year it has indicated it will do so), a kind of "modus vivendi" will have been established among Nigerians to enable them to live harmoniously and peaceably in all parts of the country. In the end, the survival of Nigeria will depend chiefly on the acceptability of any constitutional system or formula to be devised by the present Military Government and on how far Nigerians can submerge their ethnic allegiance in the interest of the entire nation.

Many of the entries are annotated, and reviews are cited for many items. Included are books, official publications, periodical and newspaper articles, conference papers, pamphlets and doctoral dissertations done specifically on the war or on related topics. The entries are classified by topic. Included are a chronology of important events related to Nigeria from pre-European times to January 15, 1970, the official end of the war; biographies of some key personalities directly or indirectly connected with the war; excerpts of the May 1966 decree promulgated by General Ironsi abolishing Regions; text of General Gowon's decree dividing Nigeria into twelve States; a list of major relief agencies; and the Nigerian national anthem. This work does not attempt to include all publications that appeared during the war, most of them ephemeral. Although they have a research value in the study of the effect of propaganda on the war, only a few representative pamphlets have been included, specifically those that may still be obtainable. There are two important documentary works published on the war to date. A. H. M. Kirk-Greene's two volume work, <u>Crisis and conflict in Nigeria: a documentary source-book, 1966-70</u> (1971), includes many important official reports, documents, proclamations, and valuable footnotes and extensive bibliography. Unfortunately, the work lacks a subject index or an index of any kind to correlate its scattered sources. The second work by Zdenek Cervenka, <u>The Nigerian Civil War; History of the War: Selected Bibliography and Documents</u> (1971), begins only with the military coup on January 15, 1966, and provides no background information on the coup itself. However, it is particularly recommended for its extensive bibliography which is arranged by topic and international in coverage.

I owe special debt of gratitude to Donald Fitch, Head of the Reference Department, University of California Library, Santa Barbara, for his editorial advice; to my brother and his wife, Dr. Jerry and Wanda Aguolu, for their valuable advice despite their heavy schedules at the University of California Medical School, at Davis; to the Rev. Dr. and Mrs. Elliot Mason of Trinity Baptist Church, Los Angeles, California, for their encouragement; to Professor Irving Lieberman, Director of the School of Librarianship, University of Washington, Seattle, for his support of my research work

## *Introduction*

in general, and to the Research Committee of the University of California, Santa Barbara, for its generous sponsorship.     I am also grateful to the following for their moral support and encouragement: Senior Magistrate S.I. Aguolu, Senior Magistrate's Court, Arochukwu, Nigeria; Basil and Eddy Lebechuku, Cooperative Division, Ministry of Trade and Industry, East Central State, Nigeria; Geoffrey and Mary Umezulike, Divisional Office, Ihiala, East Central State, Nigeria.  Nor can I fail to thank Mrs. Mary Gill for her painstaking efforts in typing and for her valuable suggestions.

September 15, 1973                         Christian C. Aguolu

# CHRONOLOGY OF IMPORTANT EVENTS

| | |
|---|---|
| 500 BC – AD 200 | The existence of the Iron Age Culture constituted by the Nok peoples – the first known culture in Nigerian prehistory. These ethnic groups, located in an area 300 miles long and 100 miles above the confluence of the Niger and Benue Rivers, are believed to be the ancestors of the contemporary ethnic groups in the area. |
| 900 – 1000 | Arab migration through Egypt into North and West Africa. |
| 1000 – 1500 | The Kingdom of Kanem flourishes. It incorporates the present State of Bornu, whose strategic and geographic position made it a convenient settlement area for the emigrants from Egypt. By the 15th century Northern Nigeria has embraced Islam, Kano becoming a center of Islamic studies and a great commercial crossroads of the Western Sudan. |
| 1237 | King of Bornu sends embassy to Tunis in North Africa. |
| 1472 | Portuguese – the first European – visit the Benin in search of slaves and palm oil. Some authorities take 1486 as the date. |
| 1553 | First English visit to Benin in quest of palm oil and slaves. |
| 1558 | First recorded export of palm oil from Benin. |
| 1796 | Mungo Park, a Scottish doctor, discovers the Niger River, informing Europe that the river flows Eastwards and not Westwards. |
| 1804 | Shehu Usman Dan Fodio, Muslim Fulani scholar and reformer, leads a successful revolt against Hausa kingdoms and sets up Fulani emirs. |
| 1807 | Britain declares slave trade illegal, preceded by Denmark in 1802 and the United States of America in 1804. |
| 1830 | Richard Lander reaches the Mouth of the Niger River at Brass. |
| 1849 | John Beecroft appointed first British Consul at Fernando Po. |
| 1851 | First Treaty signed with Lagos to stop slave trading. |
| 1861 | Britain annexes Lagos which then becomes a Crown Colony. |

# Chronology of Important Events

1879         George Taubman Goldie forms the United Africa Company by amalgamating four existing British trading firms.

1882         The United Africa Company becomes the National Africa Company.

1884-85    Berlin Conference. European Powers recognize territory around lower Niger as British.

1885         Oil Rivers Protectorate established.

1886         Colony of Lagos gets its own administration and Goldie is granted a royal charter, which authorizes his company, now renamed the Royal Niger Company, to set up an administration in the Niger River hinterland.

1893         Oil Rivers Protectorate is extended inland and then becomes the Niger Coast Protectorate.

1897         Jan. 8. The name "Nigeria" first suggested for the Niger Territories by Flora Shaw (later to become wife of Lord Lugard), African correspondent for the Times of London, and by 1900 the name is officially accepted as the proper nomenclature for the British territory.

1900         Jan. 1. The Royal Niger Company charter withdrawn and the administration of the territory formally taken over by the British Government, with Sir R. D. R. Moor as Commissioner of Southern Nigeria.

1900-1906   Sir Frederick Lugard, a former army officer and agent of the Royal Niger Company, is High Commissioner of Northern Nigerian Protectorate.

1904         Sir Walter Egerton appointed High Commissioner of Southern Nigeria.

1906         Lagos and Southern Nigeria amalgamated, becoming the Colony and Protectorate of Southern Nigeria, with Egerton as Governor.

1912         Sir Frederick Lugard appointed to the governorship of both Northern and Southern Nigeria. Coal mining begins at Enugu.

1914         The two administrations of Northern and Southern Nigeria are amalgamated and become the Colony and Protectorate of Nigeria. Sir Frederick Lugard is appointed its first Governor-General. A Nigerian Council, alongside the Lagos Legislative Council, without executive or legislative authority, is set up to advise the Governor for Lagos and the Protectorate.

1922      A Legislative Council is empowered by the Constitution to legislate for Lagos and Southern Provinces. The Governor continues to legislate for the Northern Provinces. The advisory Lagos Legislative Council in existence since 1862 and the Nigerian Council are superseded.

1923      The Legislative Council is enlarged to permit greater Nigerian representation.

1929-30      Women at Aba, Calabar, Owerri and Opobo in Eastern Nigeria riot against the British imposition of direct taxation and warrant chiefs upon the people. Many lives are lost in the riot.

1937      Dr. Nnamdi Azikiwe, an Ibo journalist, educator and orator, returns from the United States after stopping first in the Gold Coast (Ghana) for three years where he founds the newspaper, African Morning Post, serving as a springboard for nationalist agitation. Establishes a string of newspapers in Nigeria and begins to fight for what he calls "African dignity."

1946      A new constitution. Legislative authority extended to the whole of Nigeria and Regional Houses of Assembly are established to act as advisory bodies to the Central Legislature on Regional matters. The National Council of Nigeria and the Cameroons is founded by Herbert Macaulay, as President, and Nnamdi, as Secretary.

1948      University College, Ibadan, opened, affiliated with the University of London.

1949      The Northern People's Congress is founded.

1950      The Action Group formed, led by Chief Obafemi Awolowo.

1951      A Constitutional revision entrenches three Regions - North, East and West. A House of Representatives replacing the Legislative Council is provided in each Region; so is a House of Chiefs for Northern and Western Regions.

1953      Anti-Ibo riots in Kano, Northern Nigeria.

1954      Constitution amended again; more powers given to the Regions. Lagos is declared a Federal Territory and separated from the Western Region. House of Representatives is enlarged; there is a provision for the post of Governor-General to which Sir John Macpherson is appointed.

1956     Shell-British Petroleum discovers mineral oil in Eastern Nigeria after prospecting for three years.

1957     Another constitutional amendment; formation of National Government at the center and the Federal Council of Ministers. First Federal Prime Minister, Alhaji Sir Abubakar Tafawa Balewa named. Western and Eastern Regions granted self-government.

1958     First commercial shipment of mineral oil abroad.

1959     The Northern Region becomes self-governing. Federal elections held for enlarged House of Representatives. Sir Abubakar continues as Federal Prime Minister and Dr. Nnamdi Azikiwe appointed the President of the Senate, as a bicameral legislature provides for a House of Representatives and a Senate. Eastern Nigeria gains a House of Chiefs.

1960     Oct. 1. Nigeria is proclaimed an independent nation within the British Commonwealth, and Dr. Azikiwe is named the first indigenous Governor-General. University of Nigeria at Nsukka is opened.

1961     Feb. 11-12. The Northern Cameroons administered since 1922 as part of Northern Nigeria votes by a plebiscite to join Nigeria, while the Southern Cameroons chooses unification with the Cameroon Republic, becoming part of it on Oct. 1, 1961.
Oct. The University of Ife opened.

1962     Oct. University College, Ibadan, becomes independent of the University of London and is renamed University of Ibadan. The Ahmadu Bello University opened at Zaria; the University of Lagos is also opened.

1963     July 13. Mid-Western Region is created.
Sept. Chief Obafemi Awolowo and Chief Anthony Enahoro, leaders of the Action Group Party, along with other politicians are sentenced to varying terms of imprisonment for allegedly plotting to overthrow the Federal Government.
Oct. 1. Nigeria becomes a Republic (no longer recognizing Britain's Queen as Head of State). Dr. Nnamdi Azikiwe is appointed the first President of the Republic.
Nov. Census controversy; Regional Governments inflate population figures.

1964     Feb. Population of Nigeria set at 55,653,821, largest in Africa and making Nigeria the tenth most populous country in the world after China, India, the Soviet Union, the United States, Indonesia, Japan,

Pakistan, Brazil and West Germany.

<u>Dec.</u>  Boycott of national elections by Eastern, Mid-Western and Western Regions.  Movement to break up the Federation peacefully.

1965      <u>Oct.</u>  Rigged Regional elections in Western Nigeria leading to severe political crisis.  Hundreds of people killed, houses burnt.

1966      <u>Jan. 1-15.</u>  Riots in Middle-Belt of Northern Nigeria.

<u>Jan. 15.</u>  The civilian Government is overthrown in the first Nigerian military coup.  The Prime Minister, Sir Abubakar, as well as some other national leaders, is killed.

<u>Jan. 16.</u>  Major-General Aguiyi-Ironsi, Supreme Commander of the Nigerian Armed Forces, becomes Head of Federal Military Government.

<u>May 24.</u>  Federal system and Regions abolished.  Nigeria becomes simply "Republic of Nigeria"; the term "Regions" replaced by "Provinces", and Nigeria becomes virtually a unitary state.

<u>May 30.</u>  Rioting against Ibos in Northern Nigeria begins.

<u>July 29.</u>  Second  military coup.  General Aguiyi-Ironsi assassinated.  Unitary Government is abolished and the Federal system re-established.

<u>August 1.</u>  Lieutenant-Colonel (later General) Yakubu Gowon becomes Head of the Federal Military Government.

<u>Sept.-Oct.</u>  Intensified rioting against the Ibos in Northern Nigeria; thousands of them killed; survivors flee to Eastern Nigeria.  Anti-Northern feelings strong in the area, and the Military Governor, Lt.-Colonel Odumegwu Ojukwu, orders non-Easterners out of the Region.

1967      <u>Jan. 4-5.</u>  Aburi Constitutional Conference in Ghana.  The nine-point agreement falls apart in following weeks owing to differing interpretations by the Federal and Eastern Nigerian authorities.

<u>March 31.</u>  Ojukwu announces all taxes formerly collected in Eastern Nigeria by the Federal Government to be paid henceforth to the Eastern Nigerian Treasury.

<u>April 4.</u>  Federal Government imposes economic sanctions against Eastern Nigeria.

<u>May 3-26.</u>  Mass demonstrations in Enugu, Capital of Eastern Nigeria, and other Ibo towns demanding the secession of the Eastern Region from the Federation.

<u>May 26.</u>  The Consultative Assembly of Chiefs and Elders in Eastern Nigeria meets, mandating Ojukwu to declare "at early practicable date, Eastern Nigeria as a free, sovereign and independent State by the name and title of the Republic of Biafra."

<u>May 27.</u>  Gowon declares a state of emergency and decrees the creation of twelve states to replace the four existing Regions.

Eastern Nigeria declares the decree unconstitutional and inapplicable to it. The decree to take effect from April 1, 1968.

May 30. Eastern Nigeria declares itself an independent country, called "Biafra."

July 6. Civil War begins as the Federal forces invade Biafra.

July. Shell-British Petroleum, the largest oil company in Nigeria, makes a token royalty to the secessionist Government. The Federal Government blockades oil exports from Biafra, forcing oil production to a virtual standstill.

August 19. Mid-Western Region falls to the Biafran troops.

Sept. 17. Mid-Western Region secedes from the Federation and proclaims itself independent State of Benin, but is recaptured the next day by the Federal forces.

Sept. The Federal Government wins support of the Organization of African Unity meeting in Congo-Kinshasa in its effort to crush the secession.

Oct. 4. Enugu, Biafra's capital, falls.

1968

April 13. Tanzania becomes the first country to recognize Biafra (followed by Gabon on May 8, 1968; the Ivory Coast on May 14, 1968; Zambia on May 20, 1968, and Haiti on March 23, 1969).

May 19. Port Harcourt, oil port, captured by the Federal forces.

May 21. Peace talk in Uganda arranged by the Commonwealth Secretariat.

July-Sept. Starvation in the secessionist territory at the peak.

July 20. Biafran and Federal delegations at the Organization of African Unity Conference held at Niamey, Niger, arrange for formal peace talks to be held in Addis Ababa, Ethiopia.

July 31. France announces support for Biafra and calls for international action to end the war.

August 4. Peace talk in Addis Ababa ends without results.

Sept. Six Member Consultative Committee of the Organization of African Unity passes a resolution appealing for cessation of hostilities and urging the Biafrans to renounce secession and the Federal Government to grant general amnesty. Reaffirms its faith in the unity and territorial integrity of Nigeria.

Nov. Nigeria and the Soviet Union conclude a long-term economic and technical assistance pact.

1969

April 19-20. Peace talk in Monrovia, Liberia, fails.

June 6. The International Committee of the Red Cross suspends relief flights into Biafra following Nigerian shooting down of a Red Cross plane which has violated the Federal air space on June 5.

Aug. 1. Pope Paul VI makes an unsuccessful effort to resolve the conflict by inviting both sides to Kampala, Uganda, where he has gone to consecrate some African bishops.

<u>Aug. 28</u>. Dr. Nnamdi Azikiwe, former Biafran supporter, declares support for the Federal Nigeria and urges Biafrans to renounce secession and seek accommodation with the Federal Government.
<u>Nov.</u> Nigeria rejects Swiss, Austrian, Yugoslavian and Swedish proposal to mediate and reiterates that only the Organization of African Unity has jurisdiction.
<u>Dec. 16</u>. Ethiopian Emperor, Haile Selassie, invites Biafra and Federal Nigeria for a peace-talk at Addis Ababa. It fails owing to lack of agreement on the sponsorship of the talk.

1970

<u>Jan. 10</u>. Uli airstrip falls to the Federal forces. Ojukwu departs from the collapsing state.
<u>Jan. 11</u>. President Richard Nixon of the United States announces massive relief shipments to Nigeria.
<u>Jan. 12</u>. Biafran surrender – the end of the civil war.
<u>Jan. 15</u>. Biafra officially signs papers of surrender at Lagos and automatically ceases to exist, dissolving into Nigeria's East Central, Rivers and South-Eastern States in accordance with the Federal decree of May 27, 1967.

# KEY TO ABBREVIATIONS

| Abbreviations | Full Titles |
|---|---|
| Adm. Sci. Q. | Administrative Science Quarterly (New York) |
| Afr. Dev. | African Development (London) |
| Afr. Inst. Bull. | Africa Institute Bulletin (Pretoria) |
| Afr. Res. Bull. | Africa Research Bulletin (Exeter, England) |
| Afr. Stud. Rev. | African Studies Review (East Lansing, Michigan) |
| Africana Library J. | Africana Library Journal (New York) |
| Amer. Anthrop. | American Anthropologist (Washington, D.C.) |
| Amer. Hist. Rev. | American Historical Review (Washington, D.C.) |
| Amer. J. Int. Law | American Journal of International Law (Washington, D.C.) |
| Amer. J. Soc. | American Journal of Sociology (Chicago) |
| Amer. Pol. Sci. Rev. | American Political Science Review (Washington, D.C.) |
| Amer. Soc. Rev. | American Sociological Review (Washington, D.C.) |
| Atlantic. | Atlantic Monthly (Boston, Mass.) |
| Black. Acad. Rev. | Black Academy Review (New York) |
| Brit. J. Soc. | British Journal of Sociology (London) |
| Cahiers Etud. Afr. | Cahiers d'Etudes Africaines (Paris) |
| Canadian J. Afr. Stud. | Canadian Journal of African Studies (Montreal, Canada) |
| Christian Sci. Mon. | Christian Science Monitor (Boston, Mass.) |
| Commonwealth J. | Commonwealth Journal (London) |
| Cont. Rev. | Contemporary Review (London) |
| Coop. & Conflict | Cooperation and Conflict (Oslo, Norway) |
| Curr. Dig. Soviet Pr. | Current Digest of the Soviet Press (Columbus, Ohio) |
| Edit. Res. Rpts. | Editorial Research Reports (Washington, D.C.) |
| Est. Inst. | Estudios Internacionales (Santiago, Chile) |
| Geogr. Magazine | Geographical Magazine (London) |
| Govt. Opp. | Government and Opposition (London) |
| Hist. Educ. Q. | History of Education Quarterly (New York) |
| Harvard Int. Law J. | Harvard International Law International Journal (Cambridge, Mass.) |
| Illus. Lond. News | Illustrated London News (London) |
| Int. Affairs | International Affairs (London and Moscow) |
| Int. Journal | International Journal (Toronto) |
| Int. Legal Mat., Current Doc. | International Legal Materials, Current Documents (Washington, D.C.) |
| Int. Stud. | International Studies (New Delhi) |
| J. Adm. Overseas | Journal of Administration Overseas (London) |
| J. Afr. Hist. | Journal of African History (London) |
| J. Afr. Law | Journal of African Law (London) |
| J. Asian Afr. Stud. | Journal of Asian and African Studies (Leyden) |
| J. Business Soc. Stud. | Journal of Business and Social Studies (Lagos, Nigeria) |

# Key to Abbreviations

| Abbreviations | Full Titles |
|---|---|
| J. Commonwealth Pol. Stud. | Journal of Commonwealth Political Studies (Leicester) |
| J. Hum. Rel. | Journal of Human Relations (Wilberforce, Ohio) |
| J. Mod. Afr. Stud. | Journal of Modern African Studies (Cambridge, Eng.) |
| J. New Afr. Lit. Arts | Journal of the New African Literature and the Arts (New York) |
| J. Parl. Commonwealth | Journal of the Parliaments of the Commonwealth (London) |
| Keesing's Cont. Arch. | Keesing's Contemporary Archives (London) |
| L.A. Times | The Lost Angeles Times (Los Angeles, Calif.) |
| Library J. | Library Journal (New York) |
| Michigan Q. Rev. | Michigan Quarterly Review (Ann Arbor, Michigan) |
| N.Y. Rev. Bks. | The New York Review of Books (New York) |
| N.Y. Times | The New York Times (New York) |
| Negro Hist. Bull. | Negro Historical Bulletin (Washington, D.C.) |
| Nigerian J. Econ. Soc. Stud. | Nigerian Journal of Economic and Social Studies (Ibadan, Nigeria) |
| Nigerian Law J. | Nigerian Law Journal (Lagos, Nigeria) |
| Pan-African J. | Pan-African Journal (New York) |
| Pol. Sci. Q. | Political Science Quarterly (New York) |
| Pol. Stud. | Political Studies (London) |
| Quarterly Inf. Bull. Cath. Relief Services | Quarterly Information Bulletin of the Catholic Relief Services (New York) |
| Ref. Presb. World | Reformed and Presbyterian World (Geneva) |
| Rev. Déf. Nat. | Revue de Défense Nationale (Paris) |
| Rev. Est. Pol. | Revista de Estudios Politicos (Madrid) |
| Rev. Fr. Etud. Pol. Afr. | Revue Française d'Etudes Politiques Africaines (Paris) |
| Rev. Fr. Sci. Pol. | Revue Française de Science Politique (Paris) |
| Rev. Int. Comm. Jur. | Review of the International Commission of Jurists (Geneva) |
| Rev. Milit. Gén. | Revue Militaire Générale (Paris) |
| Rev. Pol. | Review of Politics (Notre Dame, Indiana) |
| Rev. Pol. Int. | Revue de la Politique Internationale (Belgrade) |
| Rev. Politica Int. | Revista de Politica Internacional (Madrid) |
| Rev. Psych. Peuples | Revue de Psychologie des Peuples (Havre, France) |
| Sat. Evening Post | Saturday Evening Post (Philadelphia) |
| Sat. Rev. | Saturday Review (New York) |
| Soc. Stud. | Social Studies (Brooklawn, New Jersey) |
| South Atlantic Q. | South Atlantic Quarterly (Durham, North Carolina) |
| T L S. | Times Literary Supplement (London) |
| Trop. Geogr. Med. | Tropical and Geographical Medicine (Haarlem, Neth.) |
| U.S. Dept. State Bull. | U.S. Department of State Bulletin (Washington, D.C.) |
| Vital Speeches | Vital Speeches of the Day (Southold, New York) |

## GENERAL STUDIES

Adler, Renata. "Letter from Biafra," New Yorker, XLV (Oct. 4, 1969), 47-113. An excellent article that provides not only the background story of the war but also delves into the war situation itself; the goals of the secessionists and the principles of their revolution. The author is former film reviewer for the New York Times.

Affia, George B. Nigerian crisis, 1966-1970: a preliminary bibliography. Lagos: Yakubu Gowon Library, University of Lagos, 1970, 24 p. Includes books and pamphlets.

Africa Research Group. The Other side of Nigeria's civil war, Boston, April 1970.

African Bibliographic Center. Nigeria and the problem of Biafra; a selected and introductory bibliographical guide, 1967-1968. Washington, D.C., 1968. 11 p. (Its current reading list series, v. 6, No. 3) A brief but excellent listing.

African Communist, London. Ten years, 1959-1969 of the African Communist. London: Unkululeko Publications (30 Goodge Street), 1969. 104 p.

Aguolu, Christian Chukwunedu. The vital issues of the Nigerian Civil War, 1967-70. Berkeley School of Librarianship, University of California, 1971-(In Progress). A detailed, analytical study which examines the historical, political and cultural factors that led to the war, the extent of the foreign involvement; relief operations; arguments for and against secession in Africa in relation to African unity and the implications of the war for Nigerians and other Africans. Its nine appendices include a chronology of important events in Nigeria from 1472 to the end of the war in 1970; select speeches by Dr. Azikiwe, Sir Abukakar, Generals Aguiyi-Ironsi and Gowon; major relief agencies; the text of the Biafran surrender and the Nigerian national anthem. Extensive bibliography, classified and annotated.

Akpan, Moses E. "African strategies in the United Nations, 1960-1966," Doctoral Dissertation, Southern Illinois University, 1970, 183 p.

Akpan, Ntieyong Udo. The Struggle for secession, 1966-1970: a personal account of the Nigerian Civil War. London: Cass, 1971. 225 p. A controversial study of the secession by a top Biafran Government official closely

(GENERAL STUDIES)

associated with it, raising the question of whether the events leading to the secession made it inevitable and whether the war itself was unavoidable after the secession, or whether in fact one could not have happened without the other. The author,
a respected Ibibio, and former Chief Secretary to former Eastern Nigerian Government, is also author of Epitaph to indirect rule: a discourse on local government in
Africa (1956) and is currently Pro-Chancellor of the University of Nigeria.

Almond, Gabriel and James S. Coleman, eds. The politics of the developing areas.
Princeton: Princeton University Press, 1960. 591 p.
Rev: Amer. J. Soc., LXVI (July 1960), 96.

Aluko, Samuel A. "Nigeria's political system: the future," New African (May 1966),
79-81

Amali, Samson O. Ibos and their fellow Nigerians. Ibadan: The Author, 1967. 55 p.
"A very personal account of the Nigerian crisis and of the role of the Ibo people in
it. It is written from the point of view of the Idoma of Benue Province, who border
Ibo country on the North." (Foreword)

Andreski, Stanislav. The African predicament: a study in the pathology of moderniza-
tion. London: Michael Joseph, 1968. 237 p.
Dealing chiefly with West Africa, it attempts to explain why the lofty hopes put on
Africa by the Western Powers have not been fulfilled, and criticizes European and
American concepts of African tribalism and nationalism. The author is Professor
and Head of the Sociology Dept., University of Reading, England.
Rev: TLS (Oct. 10, 1968), 1143.

Arikpo, Okoi. The Development of modern Nigeria. Harmondsworth: Penguin, 1967.
176 p. (Penguin African Library, AP 21)
History of Nigeria from the first European arrival; its constitutional evolution from
1914 to 1963; the emergence of nationalism; the problem of federalism, etc. Dr.
Arikpo, an anthropologist, is the Nigerian Commissioner for External Affairs.
Rev: TLS (July 13, 1967), 625.

Armand, Captain. Biafra vaincra. Paris: Editions France-Empire, 1969. 260 p.
An overly optimistic assessment of the military power of Biafra belied by the result
of the war.

(GENERAL STUDIES)

Asika, Anthony Ukpabi. <u>No victors; no vanquished: opinions, 1967-68, v. I.</u> Enugu:
East Central State Information Service, 1968. 80 p.
Interviews, speeches and writings of the Administrator of the East Central State,
a former Ibo Lecturer in Political Science at the University of Ibadan who remained
loyal to the Federal Government throughout the war.

Atilade, Emmanuel Adekunle. <u>The History of Nigerian Civil War in poems.</u> New
Nigeria Press, 1970. 24 p. (A New Africa book.)

Awolowo, Obafemi. <u>The People's Republic.</u> Ibadan: Oxford University Press, 1968.
356 p.
Critically examines the colonial rule, and reviews economic and political events
after independence, with recommendations for the improvement of Nigeria's political and economic situation. The author is former Premier of Western Nigeria and
later Leader of the Opposition in the Federal Parliament.
Rev: <u>Library J.</u>, XCIV (Dec. 1969), 4440.

_____ <u>The Strategy and tactics of the People's Republic of Nigeria.</u> London:
Macmillan, 1970. 132 p.
Analysis of economic, political and social objectives of Nigeria, with suggestions
for their attainment.
Bibliography and no index.

Azikiwe, Nnamdi. <u>Military revolution in Nigeria.</u> London: Hurst, 1973. 1550 p.?
One of the most important studies of the war by an Ibo politician, former President
of Nigeria and the architect of the Nigerian independence. His dramatic abandon-
ment of the Biafran cause in August 1969 was a grave diplomatic setback to the
Biafran secessionists and proved crucial to their surrender in January 1970.

<u>Biafra, Bilan d'une sécession.</u> (Avec une contribution de Nathan Weinstock.)
Lausanne: Ligue Marxiste Révolutionnaire, 1970. 75 p. (Brèche-documents, 2-3)
Six studies on the war.

Bonneville, Floris de. <u>Mort du Biafra.</u> Photos de Gilles Caron. Paris: R. Solar,
1968. 143 p.
Rev: <u>Conch</u>, I (March 1969), 65-8.

(GENERAL STUDIES)

Bühler, Jean. <u>Tuez-les tous! Guerre de sécession au Biafra</u>. Paris: Flammarion,
1968. 240 p.
Also published in German under the title: <u>Biafra: Tragödie eines begabten Volkes</u>,
Zurich, 1968.

Büttner, T., ed. <u>Revolution und Tradition. Zur Rolle der Tradition im anti-
imperialistischen Kampf der Völker Afrikas und Asiens</u>. Leipzig: Scientific Review
of the Karl-Marx University, 1971. 224 p.

Carter, Gwendolen, ed. <u>National unity and regionalism in eight African states</u>:
<u>Nigeria, Niger, the Congo, Gabon, Central African Republic, Chad, Uganda and</u>
<u>Ethiopia</u>. Ithaca, New York: Cornell University Press, 1966. 565 p.
Discussion by various authorities of the efforts made by the Central Government of
each country to strengthen national unity while reducing competing regional and
tribal loyalties. Bibliography follows each essay, and the essay on Nigeria provides
a useful background for understanding the first military coup in that country.
Rev: <u>Choice</u>, III (Dec. 1966), 956.
     <u>Library J.</u>, XCI (Aug. 1966), 3741.

Cayeux, J. <u>L'Agent spécial au Biafra</u>. Paris: Editions Fleuve Noir, 1968.
Rev: <u>Conch</u>, I (March 1969), 65-8.

Cervenka, Zdenek. <u>The Nigerian war, 1967-1970; history of the war, selected</u>
<u>bibliography and documents</u>. Frankfurt am Main: Bernard & Graefe Verlag für
Wehrwesen, 1971. 459 p. (Schriften der Bibliothek für Zeitgeschichte.
Weltkriegsbucherei Stuttgart. Neue Folge der Bibliographien der Weltkriegs-
bücherei, Heft I0)
The text begins with the first military coup on January I5, I966, with no background
information which is only available in the bibliography. Discusses military opera-
tions; reports of the international observers, peace efforts; the role of the Great
Powers and relief operations. Pp. 383-451, bibliography, primarily classified by
broad topics, is very international in scope.
Rev: <u>West Africa</u>, No. 2883 (Sept. 22, 1972), 1255-6.

Chapman, Audrey R. "The Relationship between the N.C.N.C. and the ethnic unions
in Mbaise, Eastern Nigeria," Paper presented at the Annual Meeting of the African
Studies Association, New York, November 1967. 18 p.

Chi. <u>Letters from Biafra</u>. Arranged and with Commentary by Betty Nickerson.

(GENERAL STUDIES)


Toronto: New Press, 1970. 159 p.


Chomé, Jules. Le Drame du Nigéria. Waterloo, Belgique: Tiers-Monde et Révolution, 1969. 79 p.


Christian Council of Nigeria. Christian concern in the Nigerian Civil War: a collection of articles which have appeared in issues of the Nigerian Christian from April 1967 to April 1969. Ibadan, 1969. 136 p.


Churchill, Winston. (Articles on Nigerian Civil War) March 3, 1969, p. 8; March 4, 1969, p. I0; March 5, 1969, p. I0; March 6, 1969, p. 8; March I2, 1969, p. 11. Times (London)
A series of articles on various aspects of the war - the background account; war situation; foreign powers; relief operations; peace efforts. See also criticism of Churchill's articles by Nigerian High Commissioner in London on p. 4 of March I0, 1969.


Collins, Robert O., ed. Problems in African history. Englewood Cliffs, N. J.: Prentice-Hall, 1968. 374 p.
The author is Professor of African History, University of California, Santa Barbara.

Collis, Robert J. Nigeria in conflict. London: Secker & Warburg, 1970. 215 p.
Dr. Collis is former Professor of Paediatrics, University of Ibadan and author of A Doctor's Nigeria (1960).
Rev: African Affairs, LXXI (Jan. 1972), 96-7.


Cousins, Norman. "Good news from Nigeria," Sat. Rev., LIII (March 14, 1970), 22.
The noted American editor of the Saturday Review at the time, a Biafran sympathizer; lauds the Federal magnanimity in victory.


Cowan, Laing Gray. The Dilemmas of African independence. Rev. ed., New York: Walker, 1968. 167 p. ist ed. 1965.
Rev: Library J., XCIII (Oct. 15, 1968), 3792.
      Soc. Stud., LX (Dec. 1969), 337.

(GENERAL STUDIES)

Critchley, J. <u>The Nigerian Civil War: the defeat of Biafra</u>. London: Atlantic Information Centre, 1970. 27 p.


Crowder, Michael and Obaro Ikime, eds. <u>West African chiefs: their changing status</u>
   <u>under colonial rule and Independence</u>. Translated from the French by Brenda
   Packman. New York: Africana Publishing Corp., 1970. 453 p.
   Selected papers of an international seminar held by the Institute of African Studies,
   University of Ife, Dec. 17-21, 1968. Includes studies of individual chiefs in both
   English- and French-speaking countries of West Africa.
   Rev: <u>Choice,</u> VIII (Sept. 1971), 888.
       <u>TLS</u> (April 30, 1971), 506.


Cruise O'Brien, Conor. "Biafra revisited," <u>N.Y. Rev. Bks</u>. (May 22, 1969), 15-27.


_____ "A Critical analysis of the Nigerian crisis," <u>Pan-African J</u>., I (Winter 1968),
   34-40.
   The Irish author, former Vice-Chancellor of the University of Ghana, is currently
   a member of Parliament in Ireland.


_____ "The Tragedy of Biafra: a condemned people," <u>N.Y. Rev. Bks</u>. (Dec. 21,
   1967), 14-20.
   Historical and political background to the war and a defense of the secession.


Daggs, Elisa. <u>All Africa: all its political entities of independence or other status</u>.
   New York: Hastings House, 1970. 824 p.
   Discussion of history, geography, economy and politics of each country. Unfavora-
   bly and favorably received by scholars.
   Rev: <u>Africana Library</u> J., I (Fall 1970), 23.
       <u>Library</u> J., XCV (Aug. 1970), 2652.


Daudu, P. C. A. "Administrative stocktaking: the case of three 'Northern' States,"
   <u>Administration</u> (Ibadan) (July 1969), 301-12.


Debré, François. <u>Biafra an II</u>. Paris: Julliard, 1968. 224 p.
   Rev: <u>Conch,</u> I (March 1969), 65-8.

(GENERAL STUDIES)

De St. Jorre, John. The Nigerian Civil War. London: Hodder & Stoughton, 1972. 437 p.

_____ "Nigerian Civil War notebook," Transition (Accra), VIII (June/July 1971), 36-41.
Reviews the war propaganda, foreign aid, relief, attitudes of the winners and losers.

Diamond, Stanley. African tragedy: the meaning of Biafra. New York: Dutton, (Forthcoming).
Dr. Diamond is Professor of Anthropology at the New School for Social Research, New York.

Dillon, Wilton. "Nigeria's two revolutions," Africa Report, (March 1966), 8-14.
Political revolution - January 1966 military coup - and scientific revolution, wrought by Nigerian scientists aimed at proper utilization of Nigeria's natural resources.

Egbuna, Obi Benue. Destroy the temple: the voice of Black Power in Britain.
London: MacGibbon & Kee, 1970. 157 p.
"This book is a love-letter, perhaps the most sincere love-letter I have ever written... motivated by love which I feel for all the oppressed peoples of the world... It is a love-letter to my people, a record of my experiences so that those who will come after us will not have to run the gauntlet my generation has been through in order to learn the black-and-white facts of life." (Introduction)
The author, a Nigerian novelist and playwright, also compares racial discrimination in the United States with that in Britain.

Egwuonwu, L. A. "The Nigerian crisis: an open reply to Lindsay Barrett," Negro Digest, XIX (Jan. 1970), 92-4.
Critical of Barrett's article in the October 1969 issue of the Negro Digest concerning the problems of reconciliation in Nigeria.

El-Ayouty, Yassin. The United Nations and decolonisation: the role of Afro-Asia.
The Hague: Martinus Nijhoff, 1971. 286 p.

Ellis, William W. "National configurations and international policies; African voting in the United Nations General Assembly: a case study," Doctoral Dissertation, New York University, 1966.

(GENERAL STUDIES)

Enahoro, Peter. "Why I left Nigeria," <u>Transition</u>, VII (July 5, 1968), 27-30.
Former editor of the most prestigious Nigerian newspaper, <u>The Daily Times,</u>
defends his support of Biafra, declaring "I am not sold on the case for a
Republic of Biafra. I am a Confederalist." The author who hails from Mid-
Western Nigeria is the brother of the Federal Commissioner for Information and
Labour.


Essien-Udom, E. U. and B. J. Dudley. <u>Nigerian crisis.</u> New York: Humanities
Press, 1971? (Ibadan history series)


Felgas, Hello A. <u>Nigeria-Biafra: a major guerra entre africanos</u>. Lisbon, 1970, 89p.


First, Ruth. <u>The Barrel of a gun; political power in Africa and the coup d'état.</u>
London: Allen Lane, The Penguin Press, 1970. 500 p.
American edition under title: <u>Power in Africa</u>, by Pantheon Books, New York.
Includes a discussion of the Nigerian military coups. The author is a South
African journalist living in England.


<u>First International Conference on Biafra, December 7, 8, 1968.</u> New York:
Columbia University, 1968. Variously paged.
"The conference was called to examine the entire complicated Biafra-Nigeria
conflict and to determine what options were open to North Americans to help find a
solution." (Introduction.) Includes the transcripts of the speeches and the recommendations of the workshops presented to the conference.


Forsyth, Frederick. <u>The Biafra story</u>. Baltimore: Penguin, 1969. 236 p. (A
Penguin special).
The British journalist attempts to explain the reasons for the secession, the goals
of the Biafrans to whom he is sympathetic, and examines the role of the British
Government and the press in the conflict; relief and refugee problems; peace
conferences and the question of genocide. A readable book, which ends in 1968.


Foster, Philip. "The Nigerian tragedy; an educational perspective: an essay review,"
<u>Hist. Educ. Q.</u>, X (Summer 1970), 255-65.
Three books on Nigeria are discussed in terms of the relationships between education and politics.

(GENERAL STUDIES)

Gache, Paul. "Le Biafra: marque-t-il l'avènement du concept de nation dans le
  monde africain?" Rev. Milit. Gén., (Juin-Déc. 1969), 19-30.
  Reviews the circumstances of the secession and attempts to assess the possible role
  of an independent Biafra in Africa.

Gold, Herbert. Biafra Good-bye. San Francisco: Two-windows Press, 1970. 45 p.
  The author is a noted American novelist based in San Francisco, who has served as
  Visiting Professor of English in Cornell, Harvard and Stanford Universities.

Green, Reginald H. "A Lament for Nigeria," Mawazo, I (June 1967), 48-56.
  Examines the historical, political, and cultural factors that led to the war; the
  minority problems; and the 12 state structure.

Hatch, John Charles. Nigeria, the seeds of disaster. Chicago: Regnery, 1970.
  313 p.
  The author, former British Labour Party specialist in Commonwealth affairs and
  known for his works on the history of post-war Africa, traces the growth of Nigeria
  from its beginning up to independence. Critical of the British colonial administration for sowing the seeds of the war, he also apportions blame to the Federal
  Nigerian and Biafran leadership for their uncompromising attitudes.

  Rev: Choice, VIII (April 1971), 276.
       Library J., XCV (Nov. 15, 1970), 3905.

Himmelstrand, Ulf. Världen, Nigeria ach Biafra: Sanningen som kom bort.
  Stockholm: Aldus/Bonner, 1969. 212 p.

Honorin, Michel. Les Chemins de la mort. Paris: Julliard, 1969. 224 p.

Harris, Richard L. "The Effects of political change on the role set of the senior
  bureaucrats in Ghana and Nigeria," Adm. Sci. Q., XIII (Dec. 1968), 386-401.

Hazlewood, Arthur, ed. African integration and disintegration: case studies in
  economic and political union. London: Oxford University Press, 1967. 414 p.
  Rev: Africa Report, XIII (June 1968), 60-2.
       J. Adm. Overseas, VII (Oct. 1968), 563.

(GENERAL STUDIES)

Hoepli, Nancy L., ed. West Africa Today. New York: H. W. Wilson, 1971. 197 p. (The Reference Shelf, vol. 42, No. 6)
Consists almost entirely of excerpts from newspapers and periodicals, topically arranged, including a section on the Biafran war.

Ige, Bola. Civil war in Nigeria: a personal view; Paul Connett - The Biafran experience. Edward H. Johnson - More deaths than Vietnam. New York: World Horizons, 1969. 23 p. phonorecord. (New, the multi media album, v. 4, No. 3)
Ige, a Yoruba lawyer, reviews both the first and second military coups in Nigeria and argues in favor of Nigerian territorial integrity and unity and Connett, President of the American Committee to Keep Biafra Alive, justifies the secession of Biafra.

Ijomah, B. I. C. Nationalism and socio-political integration in Nigeria. New York: Schenkman, 1973. Textbook edition.
Dr. Ijomah is Assistant Registrar, University of Nigeria.

Kielland, Arne. Etter Biafra, Oslo: Tiden Norsk, 1969. 132 p.

Kirk-Greene, A. H. M. Crisis and conflict in Nigeria: a documentary sourcebook, 1966-1970. London: Oxford University Press, 1971. 2 v. Bibliog.
V. 1: Jan. 1966-July 1967. 459 p.
V. 2: July 1967-Jan. 1970. 528 p.
An important documentary sourcebook with numerous critical footnotes. V. II includes an outline of events in Nigeria 1966-1970 and extensive bibliography. The author is Senior Research Fellow in African Studies, Oxford University.

Legum, Colin. "Africa's wounded giant," Observer (London), Oct. 30, 1966, p. 12.
Nigeria, the largest African nation and potentially the richest, being torn apart by tribalism.

_____ "Can Nigeria escape its past?" Africa Report, XI (March 1966), 19.
An excellent article providing pointed historical and political background to the first military coup. Stresses the general dissatisfaction of Nigerians with the overthrown civilian government and the tribal suspicion against the Ironsi regime.

*Nigerian Civil War: An Annotated Bibliography*

(GENERAL STUDIES)

Legum, Colin. "Tragedy in Nigeria," Africa Report, XI (Nov. 1966), 23-4.

Lloyd, Peter. "The Traditional political system of the Yoruba." In R. Cohen and J. Middleton, eds. Comparative political systems. Garden City, New York: National History Press for the American Museum of Natural History, 1967, pp. 267-92.

Luckham, Alexander Robin. "The Nigerian military: a case study in institutional breakdown," Doctoral Dissertation, University of Chicago, 1969. 571 p.
Published in 1971 by Cambridge University Press under the title: The Nigerian military: a sociological analysis of authority and revolt, 1960-67.

Mackintosh, John, ed. Nigerian Government and politics: a prelude to the revolution. Evanston, Illinois: Northwestern University Press, 1966. 651 p.
A political history of Nigeria during the years immediately before and after independence, with some account of the military coup of January 1966. The author, lecturer in Political Science at the University of Ibadan, later became a British Member of Parliament.
Rev: New Statesman, LXXII (Aug. 5, 1966), 206.
TLS (July 14, 1966), 611.

Maloroso, Antoine. Les Mercenaires de la charité, Paris: Euredif, 1970. 256 p.

Manue, G. "La Dislocation du Nigéria," Revue des Deux Mondes, XIII (1967), 38-42.

Mbaeyi, Paul. "The Concept of tribalism," Nigerian Opinion, VII (Jan. 1971), 15-20.
An excellent article on the history of Nigerian tribalism and its impact on national politics by a Lecturer in History, University of Ife, Nigeria.

Meek, Charles Kingsley. Law and authority in a Nigerian tribe: a study in indirect rule. New York: Barnes and Noble, 1970. 372 p. First published 1937.
A study of the social institutions of the various Ibo clans designed to determine how the principles of "Indirect Rule" could be applied to Iboland. Dr. Meek, a British anthropologist, was attached to the Nigerian Government.

Melson, Robert F. "The Relationship between Government and Labor in Nigeria,"

(GENERAL STUDIES)

Docotral Dissertation, Massachusetts Institute of Technology, 1967.

Melson, Robert F. and Howard Wolpe, eds. <u>Nigeria: modernization and politics of communalism</u>. East Lansing: Michigan State University Press, 1971. 680 p.

Mendes, Joâo. <u>La Révolution en Afrique: problèmes et perspectives</u>. Paris: The Author (5 rue Auguste-Simon), 1970. 285 p.

Metrowich, F. R., ed. <u>Nigeria: the Biafran war</u>. Pretoria: The Africa Institute, 1969. 148 p. (Occasional paper, No. 23)

Mockler, Anthony. <u>Mercenaries</u>. Translated from the French. London: MacDonald, 1970. 303 p.
Originally published in French under title: <u>L'Historie mercenaire</u>, Paris: Stock, 1969.

Mok, Michael. <u>Biafra journal</u>. New York: Time-Life Books, 1969. 96 p.
A vivid but pathetic account of author's visit to Biafra, giving not only background information on the war, but also describing the military campaigns and relief operations, and the life among the Ibos. Includes excellent photographs, portraits of Federal and Biafran leaders and a chronology of events in Nigeria from independence in 1960 to December 1968 with which his account ends.

Muffett, David Joseph. "The Coups d'état in Nigeria, 1966: a study in élite dynamics," Docotral Dissertation, University of Pittsburgh, 1971. 422 p.
A study of the political situation immediately prior to the January 1966 coup; the situation immediately prior to the June 1966 rioting in Northern Nigeria, and the situation after the July 1966 counter-coup. Three crucial groups that emerge from this study are the traditionalistic elite represented by chiefs; the modernizing elite represented by the bureaucracy divided into two major segments; "degree-holding" and "non-degree holding, " and the military.

_____ "The Failure of elite-mass communication; some problems confronting the military regime and civil services of Nigeria, " <u>South Atlantic Q.</u>, LXVII (Winter 1968), 125-40.

# Nigerian Civil War: An Annotated Bibliography

(GENERAL STUDIES)

Nigeria. Federal Ministry of Information. Nigeria - a diary of independence, 1960-1970. Lagos, 1970. 64 p.

Nigeria 1965: crisis and criticism: selections from "Nigerian Opinion." Ibadan: Ibadan University Press, 1966. 130 p.
A collection of articles selected from the Ibadan periodical Nigerian Opinion covering the period just before the January 1966 military coup in Nigeria.

Nigeria 1966: revolution and reassessment. Ibadan: Ibadan University Press, 1967.

Niven, Cecil Rex. Nigeria. New York: Praeger, 1967. 268 p. (Nations of the modern world)
Part I gives a general description of the country; the early history of the different regions and the events up to January 1967. Part II is devoted to specific subjects like economics, education, health, administration, security forces, etc.
Rev: Economist, CCXLVII (June 17, 1967), 1246.

_____ The War of Nigerian unity, 1967-1970. London, Evans for the Federal Govt. of Nigeria, 1970. 175 p.
A study of the political, economic, cultural and historical factors that precipitated the war. Examines also the military campaigns, fruitless peace talks, relief operations, the use of propaganda, and the foreign involvement. Sir Rex Niven, a former colonial administrator in Nigeria, is author of several works on Nigeria and Africa in general.
Rev: African Affairs, LXXI (Jan. 1972), 96-7.

Njaka, Elechukwu N. "Igbo nationalism: old and new," Paper presented at the African Studies Association Convention, Boston, Oct. 21-24, 1970.
Examines different concepts of Igbo traditional governmental system, relating the Igbo close family unity to the origin of the concept of Pan-Africanism. The author, an Ibo, is Professor of Political Science, University of Maryland.

_____ "The Igbo political institutions and transition," Doctoral Dissertation, University of California, Los Angeles, 1970. 734 p.
The first definitive, authoritative study of the Igbo political system.

Nwankwo, Arthur Agwuncha and Samuel Ifejika. The Making of a nation: Biafra.

(GENERAL STUDIES)

London: Hurst, 1969. 361 p.
American edition under title: <u>Biafra: the making of a nation.</u>
A well documented, background study of the political, economic and cultural
factors leading to the civil war. Taking a Pro-Biafran stand, the book ends with
the proclamation of the "Republic of Biafra" and does not deal with the war situation. Appendices include official minutes of the Nigerian military leaders at Aburi,
Ghana, on January 4 and 5, 1967; the text of the proclamation of the Republic of
Biafra and Biafran national anthem. Both authors, young Ibo scholars, are now
publishing executives.
Rev: <u>Library J.</u>, XCV (July 1970), 2473.
  <u>TLS</u> (July 31, 1969), 863.

Nzimiro, Francis Ikenna. "Pre-war urbanization in Eastern Nigeria: a case study of
  urbanization in Onitsha," Paper presented at the International Seminar on Population Problems and Policy in Nigeria, University of Ife, March 1971.
  The author is Head of the Anthropology Dept., University of Nigeria.

_____ <u>Studies in Ibo political systems</u>. Berkeley: University of California Press, 1972.
  287 p.
  Focuses on four Niger states - Onitsha, Abo, Oguta and Osomari.

Obe, Peter. <u>Nigeria: a decade of crisis in pictures</u>. Lagos: Peter Obe Photo Agency,
  1971. 200 p.

O'Connell, James. "The Nigerian crisis," <u>Insight and Opinion</u> (Accra), III, No. I
  (1968), 32-8.
  Dr. O'Connell is Professor of Political Science at Ahmadu Bello University.

Oderinde, Sam. <u>Nigerian crisis publications: a preliminary bibliography</u>. Ibadan:
  Ibadan University Library, 1971-(In Progress).
  Especially valuable for its local coverage.

Ogwurike, C., <u>et al</u>. <u>The Dialectics of the Nigerian Civil War</u>. Chatham, New Jersey:
  Chatham Bookseller, 1972.
  Dr. Ogwurike is an Ibo lawyer.

Ohonbamu, O. <u>The Psychology of the Nigerian revolution</u>. Ilfracombe: Stockwell, 1969.
  224 p.
  The author is a noted Nigerian legal scholar.

(GENERAL STUDIES)

Ojukwu, Chukwuemeka Odumegwu.  The Ahiara Declaration: the principles of the
Biafran revolution.  Geneva: Markpress, 1969.  54 p.
Reviews the circumstances of the secession, justifying it, and assesses the position
of an independent Biafra in Africa and the world at large.
Rev: Canadian J. Afr. Stud., III, No. 3 (1970), 655-8.

_____  Biafra; selected speeches and random thoughts of C. Odumegwu Ojukwu; with
diaries of events.  New York: Harper and Row, 1969.  613 p.
Also published separately in 2 volumes.
V. I.  387 p.  V. II.  226 p.
This most authoritative source of information on the civil war from the standpoint of
the secessionists presents a daily record of events immediately before and during
the war, and includes many public statements, interviews and letters concerning
Biafra's position.  Problems of relief, the position of the Organization of African
Unity, the concept of Balkanization and attitudes of the Great Powers are all exam-
ined.  The Ibo author, whose utterances and writings are couched in a highly
rhetorical language, was the leader of the secessionists.
Rev: Canadian J. Afr. Stud., III, No. 3 (1970), 655-8.
     Nation, CCX (Feb. 9, 1970), 149-51.
     Sat. Rev., LIII (Jan. 31, 1970), 32-3.

"Ojukwu's lair and the girl who snared him,"  Flamingo Magazine (Special Nigerian
edition) (Dec. 1970), 6-9 (Jan. 1971), 6-9.
An important report of an interview with former Biafran leader, in the Ivory Coast,
where he reviews the goals of his fallen state, his political and military mistakes,
and the impact of the war upon Nigeria and Africa in general.

Okpaku, Joseph, ed.  Nigeria: dilemma of nationhood; an analysis of the Biafran
conflict.  New York: Third Press, 1972.  426 p.  (Contributions in Afro-American
and African Studies, No. 12.)
Comprises ten essays with differing viewpoints.  Includes two appendices - A:
Charter of the Organization of African Unity.  B: The O.A.U. Consultative Mission.

_____  "The Writer in politics; Okigbo, Soyinka and the Nigerian crisis,"  J. New Afr.
Lit. Arts (Fall 1967), 1-13.
The author is a Nigerian playwright and editor of the Journal of the New African
Literature and the Arts.  Christopher Okigbo, an Ibo poet, died fighting for Biafra;
Wole Soyinka, a noted Yoruba playwright, was incarcerated and released after a

(GENERAL STUDIES)

year for writing an article in a newspaper considered prejudicial to national interest.

Olorunsola, Victor Adeola. "Nigerian cultural nationalisms," <u>African Forum</u>, III, No. 1 (1967), 78-89.

Olusanya, G. O. "The Zikist Movement - a study in political radicalism, 1946-50," <u>J. Mod. Afr. Stud.</u>, IV (Nov. 1966), 323-33.

Oni-Orisan, B. A. <u>A Bibliography of Nigerian history: preliminary draft</u>. Zaria: Historical Society of Nigeria, 1968. 124 p.

Onwudiwe, A. <u>A Dictionary of current affairs and army take-over</u>. Onitsha: Onwudiwe & Sons, 1966. 124 p.

Otubushin, Christopher. <u>The Exodus and the return of Chief Awolowo</u>. Lagos: Pacific Printers, 1966. 46 p.
The political significance of the imprisonment of Awolowo in 1963 on his conviction on a treasonable felony charge and his release from prison in 1966 on a State pardon.

Oudes, Bruce. "The Other Nigerian war; the foreign press takes on the Federal Military Government in a storm of misunderstanding, distrust and confusion," <u>Africa Report</u>, XV (Feb. 1970), 15-17.
The role of the press during the war examined by the International Reporting Fellow at Columbia University.

Oyinbo, John. <u>Nigeria: crisis and beyond</u>. London: C. Knight, 1971. 214 p.

Panter-Brick, S. K., ed. <u>Nigerian politics and military rule: prelude to the civil war</u>. London: Athlone Press, 1970. 276 p.
Rev: <u>African Affairs,</u> LXXI (Jan. 1972), 96-7.
<u>J. Mod. Afr. Stud.</u>, VIII (Oct. 1970), 483-5.

(GENERAL STUDIES)

Parker, John. <u>To Keep Nigeria one</u>. London: Barrie & Jenkins, 1971. 256 p.


Perham, Margery. "A Letter to General Gowon," <u>Spectator</u> (Jan. 31, 1969), 132-3. The author is a noted British historian and author of numerous works on Africa.


_____ "Nigeria's civil war," In Colin Legum and John Drysdale, eds. <u>Africa Contemporary Record</u>. London: Africa Research, 1969, pp. 1-12.


_____ "Reflections on the Nigerian civil war," <u>Int. Affairs</u> (Lond.), XLVI (April 1970), 231-46.


"Relief, reconciliation, reconstruction and rape," <u>Time</u>, XCV (Feb. 2, 1970), 16-17. Massive relief supplies for the starving in former secessionist territory on its surrender; national reconciliation; repair of war damage; reports of rape committed by some federal soldiers who were later punished.


Roberts, Bill. <u>Life and death among the Ibos</u>. London: Scripture Union, 1970. 96 p. Personal narrative of the Igbo life, 1967-70 during the civil war.


Rosen, Carl Gustav von. <u>Biafra - som jag ser det</u>. Stockholm: Wahlstrom & Widstrand, 1969. 104 p. (W & W series, No. 9)


_____ <u>Le Ghetto biafrais tel que je l'ai vu</u>. Suivi du texte intégral de la déclaration d'Ahiara par C. Odumegwu Ojukwu. Intr. de John de Saint Jorre. Grenoble-Paris: Arthand, 1969. 204 p.
The author, a celebrated maverick Swedish pilot with a penchant for the underdogs, is the first known foerigner to have effectively broken the Nigerian blockade to bring relief to the secessionists. He subsequently resorted to assisting them militarily by creating for them an instant Air Force which bolstered their morale in mid-1969, thus hardening their resistance to the Federal Government.


Roskam, Karel Lodewijk and J. van der Meulen. <u>Spanningsveld Afrika, trefpunt Biafra</u>. Groningen: Wolters-Noordhoff, 1970. 89 p. Bibliog. (Eurorsbokje 1969, 4)

(GENERAL STUDIES)

Rowan, Carl T. "Nigeria's spectacular rebound," <u>Reader's Digest</u>, XCVIII (June 1971), 156-62.
An excellent article on the Nigerian speedy economic and political recovery from the war; its foreign policy and the achievements of General Gowon.

Samuels, M. A., ed. <u>The Nigeria-Biafra conflict: report of a one day conference in Washington, D. C., May 1969</u>. Washington, D. C.: Center for Strategic and International Studies, Georgetown University, 1969. 79 p.
Rev: <u>West Africa</u>, No. 2730 (Sept. 27, 1969), 1149.

Santos, Eduardo dos. <u>Vida a morte do Biafra</u>. Lisbon: Sociedad e de Expansao Cultural, 1970. 235 p. Bibliog.

Schiller, Edward. "Nnamdi Azikiwe: the man and his ideas," <u>Black Acad. Rev.</u>, I, No. 3 (1970), 11-26.
A good biography of the leading Nigerian politician chiefly instrumental in winning Nigerian independence in 1960.

Schwab, Peter. <u>Biafra</u>. New York: Facts on File, 1971.

Schwarz, Walter. <u>Nigeria.</u> London: Pall Mall, 1968. 328 p.
A political, historical and sociological survey of the Nigerian scene up to the secession of the Eastern Region and declaration of war in July 1967. This British journalist's account of the events leading to the war is one of the very few readable, objective studies of the conflict. Extensive bibliography.
Rev: <u>West Africa</u>, No. 2665 (June 29, 1968), 749.

Segal, Aaron. "External impact on African integration," <u>Africa Today</u> (Oct., Nov. 1968), 13-15.
Examines the integration and minority problems of various African countries including Nigeria.

Smock, Audrey C. <u>Ibo politics: the role of ethnic unions in Eastern Nigeria.</u> Cambridge, Mass.: Harvard University Press, 1971. 274 p.
A micro-political study of rural or urban communities in Eastern Nigeria giving special attention to the political systems of Abiriba in Bende Division and Mbaise in Owerri Division, covering the period, 1941-1966. Includes extensive bibliography.

(GENERAL STUDIES)

Rev: Choice, VIII (July 1971), 707.
  Library J., XCVI (May 1, 1971), 1631.

Smock, David R. Conflict and control in an African trade union: a study of the Nigerian Coal Miners' Union. Stanford, California: Hoover Institution Press, 1969. 170 p. (Hoover Institution Studies, 23.)
Rev: Africa, XLI (Jan. 1971), 75-7.
  African Affairs, LXX (Jan. 1971), 87-8.

_____ and Audrey C. Smock. Cultural and political aspects of rural transformation: a case study of Eastern Nigeria. New York: Praeger, 1972. 408 p. (Praeger special studies in international economics and development.)
A study of the pre-civil war Eastern Nigeria with recommendations for the reconstruction of the war ravaged areas and guidelines for development applicable to other African rural areas. Dr. David Smock, a cultural anthropologist, is former Adviser to the Eastern Nigerian Ministry of Rural Development and Dr. Audrey Smock, author of Ibo politics: the role of ethnic unions in Eastern Nigeria (1971), is a Lecturer in Political Science at the University of Ghana.

Sosnowsky, Alexandre. Biafra: proximité de la mort, continuité de la vie. Textes de S. E. le Cardinal Marty et al. Photos de Michel Burton, et al. Paris: Fayard, 1969. iv. Bibliog.
Chiefly illustrated.
Rev: Conch, I (Sept. 1969), 62-3.

Toyo, Eskor. The Working class and the Nigerian crisis. Lagos: International Press, 1967. 112 p.

Tremearne, Arthur John. Hausa superstitions and customs; an introduction to the folklore and the folk. London: Cass, 1970. 548 p. A reprint of the 1913 edition.
Rev: Africa, XLI (Jan. 1971), 80-1.

Ukpabi, S. C. "Military considerations in African foreign policies," Transition, VI, No. 31 (1967), 35-40.

(GENERAL STUDIES)

Unongo, Paul I. The Case for Nigeria. Lagos: Town and Gown Press (14A, Lagos University Rd., Yaba, Lagos, Nigeria), 1968. 163 p.


_____ Say it loud we're black and strong: a new dawn for Nigeria, the hope and pride of the blackman. Lagos: Micho Commercial Printers, 1970. 101 p.


Uwechue, Raph. L'Avenir du Biafra. Une solution nigeriane. Préf. de Léopold Sedar Senghor. Grenoble-Paris: Arthaud, 1969. 164 p. (Coll. Clefs du savoirs.) The former Biafran envoy in Paris, apparently claiming a neutral position, calls for a cessation of hostilities, and greater local autonomy for individual states within a united Nigeria - a return to the Aburi decisions of January 4-5, 1967.


_____ "Looking back on the Nigerian Civil War," In Africa '71, New York: Africana Publishing Corp., 1971. Pp. 103-12. Reviews the causes and the results of the war, stressing the impact of the foreign intervention on the conflict, and the future of the Ibos in a united Nigeria.


_____ Reflections on the Nigerian Civil War; facing the future. With forewords by Nnamdi Azikiwe and Léopold Sédar Senghor. New rev. ed. enl. New York: Africana Publishing Corp., 1971. 206 p. Azikiwe is former President of Nigeria and Senghor is President of Senegal. Appendix C contains portraits of the principal figures in the conflict. Rev: (1st ed.) Conch, I (Sept. 1969), 63-4.
       (2nd ed.) Ikenga (Nsukka), I (Jan. 1972), 118-20.
       (1st ed.) Nation, CCX (Feb. 9, 1970), 149-51.


Wolf, Jean. La Guerre des rapaces. La vérité sur la guerre du Biafra. Paris: Michel, 1969. 288 p.


Wriggins, William Howard. The Ruler's imperative: strategies for political survival in Asia and Africa. New York: Columbia University Press, 1969. 275 p. (Southern Asia Institute publication.) Rev: Library J., XCIV (Nov. 1, 1969), 4014.
       Pacific Affairs, XLIII (Fall 1970), 422.

(GENERAL STUDIES)

Zulch, Tilman and Klaus Guercke. <u>Soll Biafra über leben?</u> Dokumente, Berichte,
<u>Analysen, Kommentare</u>. Eine Dokumentation mit einen Geleitwort von Golo Mann.
Berlin: Lettner, 1969. 268 p. Illus. Bibliog.
First edition in 1968 under title: <u>Biafra Todesurteil für ein Volk</u>?

BACKGROUND TO THE WAR

Achogbuo, O. <u>Six years of Nigerian independence, 1960-1966</u>. Enugu: Modern Printing and Publishing Co., 1966. 56 p.

Adedeji, Adebayo. <u>An Introduction to Western Nigeria; its peoples, culture and system of government</u>. Ibadan: Institute of Administration, University of Ife, 1966. 121 p. Papers presented at a seminar for officials of the Federal Public Service of Nigeria, Sept. 1966.

Ademoyega, 'Wale. <u>The Federation of Nigeria from the earliest times to independence</u>. London: Harrap, 1962. 208 p. A political history with an excellent section on the rise of Nigerian nationalism. Rev: <u>TLS</u> (March 1, 1963), 158.

Afigbo, A. E. <u>The Warrant chiefs: indirect rule in South-eastern Nigeria, 1891-1929</u>. London: Longmans, 1972. 320 p. See also author's "The Native Treasury Question under the Warrant Chief System in Eastern Nigeria, 1899-1929," <u>Odu</u>, IV (July 1967), 29-43.

Ajayi, Jacob Festus. <u>Milestones in Nigerian history</u>. Ibadan: Ibadan University Press, 1962. 47 p. Surveys major events in Nigerian history based upon the broadcasts the author gave during the Nigerian independence. The four milestones are Islam, Christianity, British colonial rule, and nationalism. Dr. Ajayi, former Professor of History at the University of Ibadan, is the Vice-Chancellor of the University of Lagos.

Akintunde, J. O. "The Demise of democracy in the First Republic of Nigeria," <u>Odu</u>., IV (July 1967), 3-28. Contends that the old political system which banned tribalism and regionalism doomed the First Republic. Well documented.

Akiwowo, A. "Tribalism and nation building in Nigeria," <u>Il Politico</u> (March 1972), 79-98.

Aluko, Samuel A. <u>The Problems of self-government for Nigeria: a critical analysis</u>. Ilfracombe: Stockwell, 1955. 62 p. Dr. Aluko is an eminent Nigerian economist.

Amoda, Moyibi. "Background to the conflict: a summary of Nigeria's political history

(BACKGROUND TO THE WAR)

from 1914-1964," In Joseph Okpaku, ed. <u>Nigeria, dilemma of nationhood: an analysis of the Nigeria-Biafra conflict by Nigerian scholars</u>. New York: The Third Press, 1972, pp. 14-75.

Armstrong, Robert G. "Nigeria, 1965-67; release from old prejudices," <u>Nigerian Opinion</u>, (March 1967), 171-3.

Austin, Dennis. "The Underlying problem of the coup d'état in Africa," <u>Optima</u>, XVI (June 1966), 65-72.

Awa, Eme. "The Federal elections in Nigeria, 1959," <u>Ibadan</u>, No. 8 (March 1960), 4-7.

_____ <u>Federal government in Nigeria</u>. Berkeley: University of California Press, 1964. 349 p.
A study of the Nigerian political structure, with an analysis of the provisions of the Nigerian constitution and the functions of various organs of government.
Rev: <u>Pol. Sci. Q.</u>, LXXX (Dec. 1965), 660-3.

Awolowo, Obafemi. <u>Path to Nigerian freedom.</u> With a foreword by Margery Perham. London: Faber & Faber, 1967. 137 p.
Reprint of the 1947 edition. One of the important early pre-independence publications critical of the British colonial rule.

_____ <u>Thoughts on the Nigerian constitution</u>. London: Oxford University Press, 1966. 196 p.
Opposed to a unitary system of government, the author who wrote this book while in prison, convicted of plotting to overthrow the Federal Government, contends that the federal system is best suited for Nigeria.
Rev: <u>TLS</u>. (June 8, 1967), 507.

Ayandele, Emmanuel A. <u>The Missionary impact on modern Nigeria, 1842-1914; a political and social analysis.</u> London: Longmans, 1966. 393 p. (Ibadan history series.)
The author is Professor of History, University of Ibadan, Nigeria.

(BACKGROUND TO THE WAR)

Azikiwe, Nnamdi. <u>Choose independence in 1960 or more states; a national challenge</u>. Onitsha: University Publishing Co., 1959? 26 p.
Nigerian independence was gained in 1960 from the British, but the division of Nigeria into 12 states was effected on May 27, 1967.

_____ "Essentials for Nigerian survival," <u>Foreign Affairs</u>, XLIII (April 1965), 447-61.
The article was prompted by the farcical Federal elections of December 1964, which nearly brought Nigeria to the brink of chaos. Dr. Azikiwe, then the Nigerian President, suggested creation of more states to allay minority fears since "the central problem of federalism in Nigeria is how to coexist in harmony."

_____ "Les Origines de la guerre civile au Nigéria," <u>Rev. Fr. Etud. Pol. Afr.</u>, (Jan. 1970), 44-5.

_____ "The Realities of African unity," <u>African Forum</u>, I (Summer 1965), 7-22.

_____ "Respect for human dignity; an inaugural address," <u>Negro Hist. Bull.</u>, XXIV (March 1961), 123-9.
On the occasion of author's inauguration as Governor-General of Nigeria in 1960.

_____ <u>Tribalism; a pragmatic instrument for national unity; a lecture</u>. Aba: International Press, 1964. 37 p.
A scholarly examination of tribalism and its impact upon national politics.

_____ <u>Zik: selections from the speeches of Nnamdi Azikiwe, Governor-General of the Federation of Nigeria</u>. Cambridge: Cambridge University Press, 1961. 244 p.
Specimens of his great speeches on topics ranging from colonialism and imperialism to independence.

Baker, James K. "The Nigerian impasse," <u>African Forum</u>, II (Fall 1966), 103-8.
A critique of the All-Nigeria Ad Hoc Constitutional Conference of Sept. 1966 in Lagos, by the Executive Director of the American Society of African Culture.

Balewa, Abubakar Tafawa. "Democracy is working in Nigeria," <u>Readers Digest</u>, LXXVIII (Feb. 6, 1961), 105-11.
An overly optimistic view of the Nigerian Prime Minister belied by the subsequent political events.

(BACKGROUND TO THE WAR)

Balewa, Abubakar Tafawa. <u>Nigeria speaks: speeches made between 1957 and 1964</u>. Selected and with an introduction by Sam Epelle. Ikeja: Longmans, 1964. 176 p. French edition by Présence Africaine, Paris. 444 p.

Bamisaiye, A. "Ethnic politics as an instrument of unequal socio-economic development in Nigeria's First Republic," <u>African Notes</u>, VI, No. 2 (1971), 94-106. Includes tables and charts on population; ethnic distribution, exports, taxation, primary and higher education. The author is Research Fellow in the Institute of African Studies, University of Ibadan, Nigeria.

Baptiste, F. A. "Constitutional conflict in Nigeria: Aburi and after," <u>World Today</u>, XXIII (July 1967), 301-8. Evaluation of the Aburi meeting in Ghana on Jan. 4-5, 1967 - the last meeting to be attended by all Nigerian military leaders before the secession and the war.

_____ "The Relations between Western Region and the Federal Government of Nigeria; a study of the 1962 Emergency," Master's Thesis, Manchester University, 1965/66. Following the political chaos in Western Nigeria caused by the two major political parties in the area, the Federal Minister of Health, Dr. Majekudunmi, was appointed by the Prime Minister to administer the Region with the suspension of the Akintola Government.

Bascom, William. <u>The Yoruba of Southwestern Nigeria</u>. New York: Holt, Rhinehart & Winston, 1969. 118 p. Rev: <u>Africa</u>, XLI (Jan. 1971), 66.

Basden, George Thomas. <u>Among the Ibos of Nigeria: an account of the curious interesting habits, customs, and beliefs of a little known people by one who has for many years lived amongst them on close and intimate terms</u>. London: Cass, 1966. 321 p. A reprint of the Seeley 1921 edition. Dr. Basden, a British Bishop and geographer, lived in Eastern Nigeria for many years.

Berger, R. "Der Nigerianische Konflikt als Problem für die geistige Elite," <u>Afrika Heute</u>, Nos. 13-14 (1968), 204-6.

25

(BACKGROUND TO THE WAR)

Blitz, L. Frankin, ed. The Politics and administration of Nigerian Government.
Lagos: African Universities Press, 1965. 281 p.
Analysis of the functions of central, regional and local governments.
Rev: Economist, CCXIX (April 2, 1966), 50.

Blumenfeld, F. Y. "Tribalism vs. nationalism," Edit. Res. Rpts., II (Nov. 2, 1960), 803-21.

Bohannan, Laura and Paul Bohannan. The Tiv of Central Nigeria. London: International-al African Institute, 1953. 100 p. (Ethnographic survey, Western Africa.)

Bretton, Henry L. Power and stability in Nigeria; the politics of decolonization.
New York: Praeger, 1962. 208 p. (Books that matter.)
Rev: Amer. Pol. Sci. Rev., LVII (Sept. 1963), 713-4.
Amer. Soc. Rev., XXVIII (Aug. 1963), 643-4.

Brown-Peterside, Gally. "Why Balewa died." Africa Report, XI (March 1966). 15-17.
The Nigerian Prime Minister, Sir Abubakar Tafawa Balewa, was assassinated in the first military coup on January 15, 1966.

Burns, Alan. History of Nigeria. 7th ed. London: Allen & Unwin, 1969. 366 p.
1st ed. 1929.
A well documented study by former Governor of Nigeria on various aspects of the country - economy, religion, sociology, history, politics and geography.

Chick, John. "The Nigerian impasse," Current History, LVI (May 1969), 292-7.

Coleman, James Smoot. Nigeria: background to nationalism. Berkeley: University of California Press, 1958. 510 p.
One of the most penetrating and authoritative studies of the political history of modern Nigeria. Religious, sociological and anthropological differences among the ethnic groups are also well examined. Extensive bibliography. The author is Professor of Political Science at the University of California, Los Angeles.
Rev: Amer. Pol. Sci. Rev., LIII (Sept. 1959), 815.
Pol. Sci. Q., LXXIV (Dec. 1959), 629.

(BACKGROUND TO THE WAR)

Coleman, James Smoot, ed. <u>Political parties and national integration in tropical
Africa</u>. Berkeley: University of California Press, 1964. 730 p.
Rev: <u>Journal of Politics,</u> XXVII (Nov. 1965), 892.
<u>TLS</u> (April 15, 1964), 297.


Cook, Arthur Norton. <u>British enterprise in Nigeria</u>. Rev. enl. ed. London: Cass,
1964. 330 p. 1st ed. 1943.
Based upon author's doctoral dissertation, University of Pennsylvania, 1937, under
title: "Nigeria; a study in British imperialism."
Rev: <u>Choice</u>, II (Jan. 1966), 808.


Crowder, Michael. <u>A Short history of Nigeria</u>. Rev. enl. ed.. New York: Praeger,
1966. 416 p.
Originally published in London in 1962 under title: <u>The story of Nigeria</u>, it "attempts
to bring together in one short volume the history of the various groups that go to
make up modern Nigeria, to trace their connections with each other and to dispel the
assumption often made that before the colonial period Africans had very little
history." (Preface) The best general history of Nigeria. Professor Crowder is
former Director of the Institute of African Studies, University of Ife, Nigeria.
Rev: <u>Choice</u>, IV (May 1967), 330.


_____ <u>West Africa under colonial rule</u>. London: Hutchinson, 1968. 560 p.
Evaluates the benefits of colonial rule, contending that it was necessary for the
African integration into the modern world.
Rev: <u>West Africa</u>, No. 2674 (Aug. 31, 1968), 1013-5.


_____ ed. <u>West African resistance: the military response to colonial occupation</u>.
New York: Africana Publishing Corp., 1971. 314 p.
Rev: <u>Library J.</u>, XCV (Dec. 1, 1970), 4170.


_____ and Obaro Ikime, eds. <u>West African chiefs: the changing status under colonial
rule and independence</u>. Trans. from the French by Brenda Packman. New York:
Africana Publishing Corp., 1970. 453 p.
Selected papers of an international seminar held by the Institute of African Studies,
University of Ife, Dec. 17-21, 1968. Twenty-one contributors survey chieftaincies
in English and French West Africa, analyzing the position of individual chiefs
within the political structure of their countries before and after independence.

(BACKGROUND TO THE WAR)

Rev: <u>Choice</u>, VIII (Sept. 1971), 888.
<u>TLS</u> (April 30, 1971), 506.

Dada, R. A. <u>Les Origines de la guerre civile du Nigéria. De la colonisation à la</u>
<u>sécession biafraise</u>. Bruxelles, Université de Bruxelles, 1969. 140 p.

Diamond, Stanley. <u>Nigeria: model of a colonial failure</u>. With discussions by Simon
Obi Anekwe and others. New York: American Committee on Africa, 1967. 88 p.
(Occasional paper 6.)
Comprises author's articles taken from various scholarly journals, providing the
economic, historical and political background to the fall of the First Nigerian
Republic. The accompanying discussions indicate Nigerians' reactions to Professor
Diamond's arguments. The author conducted an extensive anthropological field
work in Nigeria's Middle Belt, 1958-1959.

_____ "The Trial of Awolowo: a Nigerian tragedy," <u>Africa Today</u>, X, No. 9 (1963),
22-8.
The trial of Chief Obafemi Awolowo, former Premier of Western Nigeria, on the
charge of treasonable felony in 1962, of which he was convicted and imprisoned,
constituted a chain of events leading to the civil war.

_____ "The Weight of the North," <u>Africa Today</u>, X, No. 1 (1963), 4-5, 15.
The political impact of the disproportionately large size of Northern Nigeria upon
the national politics under the Nigerian constitution.

"Did the Empire end too soon?" <u>Manchester Guardian</u>, Jan. 24, 1970. p. 1.
Critical of the British colonial policy.

Dike, Kenneth Onwuka. <u>Trade and politics in the Niger Delta, 1830-1885: an introduc-</u>
<u>tion to the economic and political history of Nigeria</u>. Oxford: Clarendon Press,
1956. 250 p. (Oxford studies in African affairs.)
The author, a prominent Nigerian historian, is Professor of African History,
Harvard University.

Dubula, Sol. "Nigeria in turmoil," <u>African Communist</u>, XXXVI (1968), 46-56.

(BACKGROUND TO THE WAR)

Dudley, Billy J. "Nigeria sinks into chaos," Round Table, LVII (Jan. 1967), 42-7.

_____ "Nigeria's civil war; the tragedy of the Ibo people," Round Table, LVIII (Jan. 1968), 28-34.

_____ Parties and politics in Northern Nigeria. London: Cass, 1968. 352 p.
Revision of author's doctoral dissertation, London University, 1965/66, it examines the power structure in Northern Nigeria, noting that the slow rate of development of modern politics in the area has been chiefly due to comparative lack or retarded rate of Western style education.
Rev: West Africa, No. 2687 (Nov. 30, 1968), 1409-10.

_____ "Traditionalism and politics: a case study of Northern Nigeria," Govt. Opp., II (July/Oct. 1967), 509-24.

Ejindu, Dennis D. "Major Nzeogwu speaks," Africa and the World, (May 1967), 14-16.
Major Nzeogwu, an Ibo from Mid-Western Nigeria, led the first military coup on January 15, 1966. He later died fighting for Biafra in the early period of the war.

Ekechi, F. K. "Colonialism and Christianity in West Africa: the Igbo case, 1900-1915," J. Afr. Hist., XII, No. 1 (1971), 103-15.

Ekpebu, Lawrence. "Background to the Nigerian crisis," Research Review (Lagos) (1969), 2, 33-60.

Ekpeyong, J. W. Nigerian crisis; the root cause. Lagos: Calabar-Ogoja Provincial Community, 1967. 24 p.

Enahoro, Anthony. Fugitive offender; the story of a political prisoner. London: Cassell, 1965. 436 p.
Written in prison, it records the circumstances of author's arrest, trial and conviction on treasonable felony charge, and reviews the pros and cons of one party system; the concept of African unity. The author, former Deputy Leader of the Action Group, and former editor of a leading Nigerian newspaper, is currently

(BACKGROUND TO THE WAR)

Nigerian Commissioner for Information and Labour.
Rev: <u>Cont. Rev.</u>, CCVIII (March 1966), 168.
    <u>Economist,</u> CCXVIII (Jan. 15, 1966), 206.


Essien-Udom, E. U. "Two elections in Nigeria, 1964 and 1965," Paper presented at
the Conference on Democratic Idea on Transitional Societies, sponsored by the
Social Science Research Council, Rome, April 1966.
Both elections, Federal and West Regional, were farcical, the latter creating the
political impasse in Western Nigeria which brought in dissatisfied military elements
in the Federal Army to end the civilian regime in January 15, 1966. The author is
Professor of Political Science, University of Ibadan, Nigeria.


<u>Events: a diary of important happenings in Nigeria from 1960-1967.</u> 2nd ed. Lagos:
Orbit Publications, 1968. 114 p. Cover title: <u>Day to day events in Nigeria, 1960 to</u>
<u>1967.</u>


Ezenwa, Vincent. "Why Nigeria burst up," <u>African Monthly Review</u> (Aug. 1967), 6-9.


Ezera, Kalu. <u>Constitutional development in Nigeria: an analytical study of Nigeria's</u>
<u>constitution-making development and the historical and political factors that affected</u>
<u>constitutional change.</u> 2nd ed. Cambridge: Cambridge University Press, 1964.
316 p.
Constitutional history of Nigeria based upon the author's doctoral dissertation,
Oxford University, 1957/58, under title: Constitutional developments in Nigeria,
1944-1956."
Rev: <u>African Forum,</u> I (Fall 1965), 122-4.


_____ "Constitutional government and democracy in Nigeria," <u>J. Parl. Common-</u>
<u>wealth,</u> XLIII (July 1962), 232-8.


Fadahunsi, Olushola. <u>Nigeria; the last days of the First Republic.</u> Lagos, 1971.
85 p. (Forthcoming.) (When published, available at University of Ife Bookshop, Ltd.,
Ibadan Branch, Ibadan, Nigeria.)


"The Fall of the Fulani Empire," <u>South Atlantic Q.</u>, LXVII (Autumn 1968), 591-602.

(BACKGROUND TO THE WAR)

The century old, highly centralized empire was eventually broken up in 1967 by the Federal State decree, splitting Northern Nigeria into six states.

"Famine and slaughter in Africa: the story behind Biafra's war," U.S. News & World Report, LXV (July 22, 1968), 38-9.

Feit, Edward. "Military coups and political development; some lessons from Ghana and Nigeria," World Politics, XX (Jan. 1968), 179-93.

Ferguson, John. The Yorubas of Nigeria. Bletchley: Open University Press, 1970. 82 p.
The author is former Professor of Classics, University of Ibadan, Nigeria.

Flint, John E. Nigeria and Ghana. Englewood Cliffs: Prentice-Hall, 1966. 176 p.
(A spectrum book. The modern nations in historical perspective, S-618.)
A comparative study of the political history of the former British colonies. The author is former Professor of History at the University of Nigeria.
Rev: J. Afr. Hist., VIII, No. 3 (1967), 541-6.

"General Ironsi's trust in his friends leads Nigeria back to tribal strife," Guardian (Manchester), June 25, 1966. p. 9.
Claims that General Ironsi's appointment of his trusted friends and other Ibos to important Federal posts revived the charge of tribalism levelled against the toppled civilian government.

Harris, Richard L. "Crisis and compromise," Africa Report, X (March 1965), 25-31.
The controversial national elections of 1964 nearly caused the break-up of the coun-try. A hasty compromise, struck by the national leaders, still left the basic problems unresolved.

Hatch, John. "The Dissolution of Nigeria," New Statesman, LXXIII (June 2, 1967), 750.

# Nigerian Civil War: An Annotated Bibliography

(BACKGROUND TO THE WAR)


Hatch, John. "Nigerian brinkmanship," New Statesman, LXXI (June 17, 1966), 869.


Huntington, Samuel Phillip. "Political development and political decay," World
Politics, XVII (April 1965), 386-430.


_____ Political order in changing societies. New Haven: Yale University Press,
1968. 488 p.
Rev: Amer. Soc. Rev., XXXIV (Aug. 1969), 571.


Institute of Commonwealth Studies, London. Opposition in the new African states.
London: Institute of Commonwealth Studies, University of London, 1969. 129 p.
(Collected seminar papers series, No. 4.)


_____ Post-independence constitutional changes. London: Institute of Commonwealth
Studies, University of London, 1969. 138 p. (Collected seminar papers, No. 5.)


Isola-Osubu, K. "Confusion in Nigeria," Africa and the World, No. 5 (Feb. 1965),
6-9.


Jakande, Latif Kayode. The Trial of Obafemi Awolowo. Lagos: John West Publications, 1966. 354 p.
This trial of former Leader of the Opposition in the Nigerian Federal Parliament
along with other 28 members of his political party, the Action Group, on the charge
of treasonable felony ended in their convictions after eleven months. Awolowo,
sentenced to ten years imprisonment on Sept. 11, 1963, was granted a State pardon
and released in 1966.


Kapil, Ravi L. "On the conflict potential of inherited boundaries in Africa," World
Politics, XVIII (July 1966), 656-73.


Kerri, J. N. Language - a factor in Nigeria's disintegration. Uppsala: Scandinavian
Institute of African Studies, 1969. 31 p. (mimeographed).


32

(BACKGROUND TO THE WAR)

Kilson, Martin. "Behind Nigeria's revolt (Jan. 15, 1966); tribal power struggle," New Leader, (Jan. 31, 1968), 9-12.


Kirk-Greene, A. H. M. Lugard and the amalgamation of Nigeria; a documentary record. London: Cass, 1968. 281 p.
Rev: Economist (Jan. 4, 1969), 36.


_____ "The Peoples of Nigeria: the cultural background to the crisis," African Affairs, LXVI (Jan. 1967), 3-11.
An abridged version of a talk given at a joint meeting of the Royal African Society with the Royal Commonwealth Society on Nov. 3, 1966, presided over by Sir James Robertson, former Governor-General of Nigeria.


Klineberg, Otto and Maris Zavolloni. Nationalism and tribalism among African students: a study of social identity. Paris: Mouton, 1969. 324 p. (International Social Science Council, No. 2.)


Langa, A. "Nigeria: behind the coup," African Communist (London), No. 25 (1966), 68-78.
Nigeria's first military coup on January 15, 1966.


Legum, Colin. "Tragedy in Nigeria; massacre of the proud Ibos," Observer (London) Oct. 16, 1966, p. 12.
The rioting against and killings of thousands of Ibos living in Northern Nigeria were the basic cause of the secession.


Lewis, Primila. "Tribalism must die - an African verdict," Atlas, XVI (Dec. 1968), 46-7.
A truly democratic state cannot be created in Africa owing to intense tribal attachments.


Lloyd, Peter C. "The Ethnic background to the Nigerian crisis." In S. K. Panter-Brick, ed. Nigerian politics and military rule; prelude to the civil war. London: Athlone Press, 1970, pp. 1-13.

(BACKGROUND TO THE WAR)

Mba, A.  From the start to surrender; the story and records of Nigerian Civil War for unity; including current affairs of the twelve States Cabinet.  Onitsha, 1971. 52 p. (Forthcoming. )  (When published available at the University of Ife Bookshop Ltd. , Ibadan Branch, Ibadan, Nigeria. )

Mackintosh, John P.  "Electoral trends and the tendency to one party system in Nigeria, " J.  Commonwealth Pol.  Stud. ,  I  (Nov. 1962),  194-210.

_____  "Nigeria since independence, " World Today,  XX  (Aug. 1964),  328-37.

_____  "Politics in Nigeria; the Action Group crisis of 1962, "  Pol.  Stud. ,  XI (June 1963),  126-55.

_____  "The Struggle for power in Nigeria, "  Transition,  (Kampala),  V,  No. 22 (1965),  21-5.

Meisler, Stanley.  "Break-up in Nigeria; roots of the civil war, "  Nation,  CCV (Oct. 9, 1967),  334-6

Mortimer, Molly.  "Voting in Nigeria, "  Cont.  Rev. ,  CCVI (Jan. 1965),  18-20.

Nicolson, I.  F.   The Administration of Nigeria, 1900-1960: men, methods and myths. Oxford: Clarendon Press, 1969.  326 p.
Rev: J.  Mod.  Afr.  Stud. ,  IX (May 1971),  153-6.

Nigeria.  Origins of the Nigerian Civil War, by Nnamdi Azikiwe, former President of Nigeria, Lagos, 1969?  17 p.
One of the most important writings on the political, historical, economic and cultural factors that led to the war by the architect of the Nigerian independence, perhaps the most knowledgeable person about Nigerian politics.  Although he claims an absolute objectivity, (which he is for the  most part of the booklet, ) he contends that Eastern Nigeria, by breaking away from the Federation, violated section 86 of the Nigerian Constitution which forbade any Region to secede from the Central Government, and blames the Biafran leadership for the "misery, desolation, death

(BACKGROUND TO THE WAR)

and tragedy" brought to their people. This was apparently written after the former President of Nigeria had thrown up his support of the secession.

Nigeria. Embassy. Nigerian record: background notes on the events in the Federal Republic of Nigeria. Washington, D. C., 1968.
Three publications in a series.
No. 1: Creation of states.
No. 2: Record of a rebel.
No. 3: Unity or disintegration?

Nigeria. Federal Ministry of Information. Nigeria, 1966: events in Nigeria in 1966, and policies and objectives of the Federal Military Government. Lagos, 1967. 61 p.

Nigeria. State House. Sixteen days of political crisis... Lagos, Federal Ministry of Information, 1965. 7 p.
The statement of Nigerian President, Dr. Nnamdi Azikiwe, on the 1964 election crisis.

Nigeria, Eastern. Ministry of Information. The Ad hoc conference on the Nigerian constitution. Enugu: Govt. Printer, 1966. 145 p. (Nigerian crisis 1966, vol. 4.)

_____ Jan. 15 (1966); before and after. Enugu: Govt. Printer, 1967. 91 p.
The first Nigerian military coup occurred on January 15, 1966.

_____ Nigerian crisis, 1966. Enugu, 1966. 68 p.
The viewpoint of the Eastern Nigerian Government.

_____ Nigerian pogrom; the organized massacre of Eastern Nigerians. Enugu, 1966. 73 p. ("Crisis" series, vol. 3.)
Rioting in Northern Nigeria which resulted in the deaths of thousands of Eastern Nigerians, May-October, 1966.
_____ The North and constitutional developments in Nigeria. Enugu: Govt. Printer, 1967. 40 p.

(BACKGROUND TO THE WAR)

Nigeria, Eastern. Ministry of Information. The Problem of Nigerian unity; the case of Eastern Nigeria. Enugu: Govt. Printer, 1966. 50 p.


_____ Summary of inhuman actions by Northern Nigeria against Eastern Nigeria. Enugu, 1967. 4 p.


_____ Thirty-nine accusations against Nigeria. Enugu, 1967. 10 p.


Nigeria, Mid-Western. Military Governor's Office. Our stand: survival and unity of the Federation; statement by the Military Governor, Lt. Colonel D. A. Ejoor. Benin City: Ministry of Internal Affairs and Information, 1966. 22 p.


Nigeria, Western. Military Governor's Office. Nigerian situation; our stand in the West; broadcast to the people of Western Nigeria by His Excellency the Military Governor, Col. R. A. Adebayo, on 1st March, 1967.
Ibadan: Ministry of Home Affairs and Information, 1967. 16 p.
Text in English and Yoruba.


"Nigeria." In Colin Legum and John Drysdale, eds. Africa contemporary record.
Exeter: Africa Research Ltd., 1970, pp. 543-83.
Reviews the events that led to the war, Nigeria's economic potentialities, foreign policy and future.


Nwankwo, M. R. The Bitterness of politics and Awolowo's last appeal.
Onitsha: A. Onwudiwe, 1965. 106 p.
Awolowo's appeal to the Federal Supreme Court on his conviction on a charge of treasonable felony in September 1963 was rejected and his prison term of ten years was reaffirmed.


Nzegwu, Henry. "Hidden facts about January coup," African Monthly Review (Sept. 1967), 12-13.
The first Nigerian military coup of January 15, 1966.


O'Connell, James. "The Anatomy of a pogrom; an outline model with special

(BACKGROUND TO THE WAR)

reference to the Ibo in Northern Nigeria," <u>Peace</u>  (July 1967), 95-100.
The author is former Professor of Political Science, University of Ibadan, Nigeria.


_____  "The Ibo massacres and secession," <u>Venture</u>  (July 1969), 22-5.


_____  "The Scope of the tragedy," <u>Africa Report</u>, XIII  (Feb. 1968),  8-12.
Reviews the political situation before and during the military coups of 1966, and offers suggestions for the political settlement of the conflict.
Odumosu, Oluwole Idowu. <u>Constitutional crisis: legality and President's conscience.</u>
Lagos: Printed for the author by Ajanlekoko Printing Works, Ibadan, 1965. 53 p.
The author is Professor of Law at the University of Ife, Nigeria.


Offonry, H. Kanu.  "The Strength of Ibo clan feeling," <u>West Africa,</u>  No. 1787  (May 26, 1951),  467; No. 1788  (June 1951),  489-90.


Okpara, Michael I.  "Pragmatic African socialism,"  Lecture delivered to the Undergraduates of the University of Ife, Ibadan, Nigeria, 1965.
Dr. Okpara is former Premier of Eastern Nigeria and Leader of the N. C. N. C., one of the major political parties in Nigeria now banned.


Olisa, Michael S.  "Political culture and stability in Igbo society," <u>Conch</u>,  III  (Sept. 1971),  16-29.


_____  "Tradition and change in Nigerian political development," Doctoral Dissertation, Cambridge University, 1964.


Olorunsola, Victor.  "Nigerian cultural nationalisms," <u>African Forum</u>,  III  (Summer 1967),  78-89.


"1966 massacre of the Ibos being played down," <u>L. A.  Times</u>,  Sept. 21, 1969, Section A, p. 12.
Opponents of the secession reject the figure of 30,000 for the Ibos killed in Northern Nigeria during the 1966 rioting in the area but indicate about 5,000 people were slain.

*Nigerian Civil War: An Annotated Bibliography*

(BACKGROUND TO THE WAR)

Onipede, F. Oladipo. "Nigerian plural society: political and constitutional development, 1870-1954," Doctoral Dissertation, Columbia University, 1956. 389 p.

Onyenwu, Okachi. "Nation-building in Nigeria, 1900-1950," Doctoral Dissertation, American University, Washington, D.C., 1967.

Orr, Charles William. The Making of Northern Nigeria. With a new introduction by A. H. M. Kirk-Greene. 2nd ed. London: Cass, 1965. 306 p. 1st ed. 1911, by Macmillan.
A study of the foundation and consolidation of the British rule in Northern Nigeria.

Ottenberg, Simon. Double descent in an African society: the Afikpo village group. Seattle: University of Washington Press, 1968. 284 p. (American Ethnological Society, monograph 47.)
Traces the origin of the Ibo village-group of Afikpo and shows how each era has influenced or been affected by double descent as opposed to the prevailing unilineal descent systems in Africa. Extensive bibliography and index. The author is Professor of Anthropology, University of Washington, Seattle.

_____ "The System of authority of the Afikpo Ibo of Southeastern Nigeria," Doctoral Dissertation, Northwestern University, 1957.

Pilkington, Frederick. "The Problem of unity in Nigeria," African Affairs, LV (July 1956), 219-22.

"Die Politischen, ethnischen und religiosen Hintergrunde der nigerianische Krise," Herder-Korrespondenz, No. 3 (Jan. 22, 1968), 136-41.

Post, K. W. J. "The Crisis in Nigeria," World Today, XXII (Feb. 1966), 43-7.

_____ The Nigerian federal election of 1959; politics and administration in a developing political system. London: Oxford University Press for the Nigerian Institute of Social and Economic Research, 1963. 518 p.
Rev: Pol. Stud., XI (Oct. 1963), 330-2.

# Nigerian Civil War: An Annotated Bibliography

(BACKGROUND TO THE WAR)

Post, K. W. J. "Revolt in Nigeria," Round Table., LVI (July 1966), 269-73.


Saidu, M. "La Crise nigérianne," Tam-Tam (Feb. 1969), 24-6.


Sale, J. K. "Redrawing the map of Africa," War/Peace Report, IX (March 1969), 12-14.
Inherited colonial boundaries drawn up by the colonial masters to suit their interest are the major source of tribal unrest in Africa.


Sampson, Eldon F. Nigeria; tribalism versus nationalism, a research report presented to the Faculty. Maxwell Air Force Base, Alabama, Air University, 1969.
Microfilm copy of typescript made by Stanford University, Photographic Dept. 72 p. map.


Schwartz, Frederick A. Nigeria: the tribes, the nation, or the politics of independence. Cambridge, Mass.: M.I.T. Press, 1963. 316 p.
Rev: N.Y. Rev. Bks., V (Dec. 23, 1965), 24.


Schwarz, Walter. "Eastern Nigeria defies Lagos on states," Guardian (Manchester), (May 30, 1967). p. 8.
The Federal decree of May 27, 1967, dividing the country into twelve states disregarded by Eastern Nigeria in its proclamation of independence on May 30, 1967.


_____ "Tribalism and politics in Nigeria," World Today, XXII (Nov. 1966), 460-7.
The impact of ethnic or regional loyalties upon Nigerian politics.


_____ "Tribalism in Nigerian universities," Guardian (Manchester), July 31, 1965, p. 9.
Charges of tribalism in appointments in the Universities of Ibadan and Lagos.


Seeburg, Gustav. Die Wahrheit über Nigeria/Biafra. Vorgeschichte und Hintergrunde des Konfliktes. Berne: Haupt, 1969. 135 p.


Seibel, H. D. "Interethnische Beziehungen in Nigeria," Soziale Welt, IV (1967),932-43.

# Nigerian Civil War: An Annotated Bibliography

(BACKGROUND TO THE WAR)

Sertorio, G. "L'Evoluzione constituzionale della Nigeria," Africa (Rome), XIX (July/Sept. 1964), 120-32.
Constitutional evaluation of Nigeria from 1914 to the attainment of the Republican status in October 1963.
_____ "Il Nazionalismo nigeriano," Politico, XXIX (Oct. 1964), 932-43.


Skinner, David Elmo. "The Influence of ethnic diversity on the development of political party systems in Burma and Nigeria," Master's Thesis, University of California, Berkeley, 1964. 93 p.


Sklar, Richard L. "The Contributions of tribalism to nationalism in Western Nigeria," J. Hum. Rel., VIII (Spring/Summer 1960), 407-18.
Dr. Sklar is Professor of Political Science at the University of California, Los Angeles.
_____ "Contradictions in the Nigerian political system," J. Mod. Afr. Stud., III (Aug. 1965), 201-13.
A lucid analysis valuable in understanding the eventual fall of the first Nigerian Republic.
_____ Nigerian political parties; power in an emergent African nation. Princeton: Princeton University Press, 1963. 578 p.
"Concerned with the development of the Nigerian political system during the final decade of the British colonial rule. The core of its analysis is the social composition and construction of those parties which stood at the forefront of the movement for independence." (Preface)
Includes extensive bibliography.
Rev: Amer. Pol. Sci. Rev., LVIII (Sept. 1964), 726-7.


_____ "Nigerian politics: the ordeal of Chief Awolowo, 1960-65." In Gwendolen Carter, ed. Politics in Africa, 7 cases. New York: Harcourt, Brace & World, 1966, pp. 119-63.


_____ and C. S. Whitaker. "The Federal Republic of Nigeria." In Gwendolen Carter, ed. National unity and regionalism in eight African states. Ithaca, New York, Cornell University Press, 1966, pp. 7-150.
An excellent essay on the history of Nigerian political parties and their social organization; impact of ethnic diversity on them; Nigeria's foreign policy, etc.
Extensive bibliography on pp. 137-50 is topically classified.

(BACKGROUND TO THE WAR)

Smith, Thomas. Elections in developing countries: a study of electoral procedures used in Tropical Africa, South-East Asia and the Caribbean. London: Macmillan, 1960. 278 p.

Stokke, O. "Tensions in the Nigerian political system before the Civil War," Internasjonal Politikk (Oslo), Nr. 3 (1969), 313-51. In Norwegian with English summary.

Tilman, Robert O. and Taylor Cole, eds. The Nigerian political scene. Durham, North Carolina: Duke University Press for the Duke University Commonwealth Studies Center, 1962. 340 p. (Duke University Commonwealth Studies Center. Publication, No. 17.) Rev: Pol. Stud., XI (Oct. 1963), 330-2.

Torres, A. "La Guerre au Nigéria," Esprit. (Dec. 1969), 807-16.

Toyo, E. "Nigeria: causes of a crisis," Tricontinental (Havana), No. 12 (1969), 34-52.

"Tribalism tears at nations of black Africa," N.Y. Times, Nov. 23, 1969, pp. 1 & 24. Tribal antagonisms responsible for African political instability.

"Tribalism versus democracy," Guardian (Manchester), Nov. 12, 1969, p. 10. Tribalism viewed as a grave obstacle to the creation of democratic state in Africa.

Uchendu, Victor Chikezie. The Igbo of Southeast Nigeria. New York: Holt, Rinehart and Winston, 1965. 111 p. (Case studies in cultural anthropology.) Bibliog. Analytical study of various aspects of Igbo traditional life - religion, family system, marriage, political and social organization, etc. Dr. Uchendu is an Igbo anthropologist teaching at Stanford University.

_____ "Status and hierarchy among the Southeastern Igbo," Master's Thesis, Northwestern University, Evanston, Illinois, 1963.

*Nigerian Civil War: An Annotated Bibliography*

(BACKGROUND TO THE WAR)


Ukpabi, Sam C.  Military involvement in African politics: a historical background. New York: The Conch Magazine, 1972.  (Conch African monograph series.)


Unongo, Paul.  "The Genesis of the Nigerian Civil War," Nigerian Journal (New York) I (Dec. 1, 1968).


Uwanaka, Ch. U.  Awolowo and Akintola in political storm.  Yaba: J. Okwesa for the Author, 1963.  119 p.
Chief Samuel Akintola, Premier of Western Nigeria, was killed in the first Nigerian military coup on January 15, 1966, following the blatantly corrupt elections conducted by him and his political party.  He and Chief Awolowo, both Yorubas, and leaders of the major political parties in Western Nigeria, were bitter political enemies.


Van de Walle, Etienne.  "Who's who and where in Nigeria; the latest available figures on population and tribal distribution," Africa Report, XV (Jan. 1970), 22-3.
Indicates how the unreliability of and controversy over Nigerian census contributed to the break-up of the First Nigerian Republic and to the Civil War.  Includes statistical tables.


Vickers, M.  "Background to breakdown in Nigeria: the Federal election of 1964-65," Africa Quarterly (New Delhi), VII, No. 2 (1967), 106-24.


_____  "Competition and control in modern Nigeria: origins of the war with Biafra," Int. Journal (Summer 1970), 603-33.


Walton, E.  "Things fall apart; the Nigerian dilemma in perspective," Negro Digest (July 1967), 31-3.


Williams, David.  "Democracy's hopes in Nigeria," Times (London), Jan. 22, 1965, p. 13.
The effect of the corrupt Federal elections of December 1964 on Nigeria.

FEDERALISM, CONFEDERALISM, AND MINORITY PROBLEMS

Abernethy, David. "Nigeria creates a new Region." <u>Africa Report</u>, IX (March 1964), 8-10.
Creation of the Mid-Western Region comprising the Provinces of Benin and the Delta in 1963 by the Federal Government after ascertaining the wishes of the people in the areas through a plebiscite.

Adedeji, Adebayo. <u>Federalism and development planning in Nigeria</u>. Ibadan: Nigerian Institute of Social and Economic Research, 1969. 45 p. (Conference on national reconstruction and development in Nigeria, paper 5.)

_____ "Federation, economic planning and plan administration in national reconstruction and development in Nigeria," Seminar paper, Ibadan, 1969.

Akintunde, J. O. "Das Ableben der Demokratie in der Republik von Nigeria," <u>Afrika Heute</u>, No. 12 (1969), 180-6.

Alberich, J. C. "Secesión en la Federación de Nigeria," <u>Rev. Politica Int.</u>, 92 (July/Aug. 1967), 149-62.

Anber, Paul. "Modernization and political disintegration: Nigeria and the Ibos," <u>J. Mod. Afr. Stud.</u>, V (Sept. 1967), 163-79.

Anise, Emmanuel O. "The Impact of the federal structure and party system on political integration in Nigeria, 1946-1970," Doctoral Dissertation, Syracuse University, 1970. 656 p.
Stressing the fact that the creation of a truly Nigerian nation-state is impossible owing to the British colonial administrative pattern and decolonizing process within a multi-ethnic, culturally heterogeneous nation like Nigeria.

Armstrong, Robert G. <u>The Issues at stake, Nigeria 1967</u>. Ibadan: Ibadan University Press, 1967. 17 p.

_____ "The Nigerian Federation," <u>Nigerian Opinion</u>, III, Nos. 5-6 (1967), 201-2.

(FEDERALISM, CONFEDERALISM AND MINORITY PROBLEMS)

Asika, Anthony Ukpabi. "Why I am a Federalist," <u>Transition</u>, VIII, No. 36 (1968), 39-44; <u>Insight</u> (Lagos), (Oct. 1968), 7-14.
An interview with the Ibo administrator of the East Central State who remained loyal to the Federal Government during the war.

Awa, Eme. "Regionalism in Nigeria," Doctoral Dissertation, New York University, 1955.

Azikiwe, Nnamdi. <u>I believe in one Nigeria-Zik</u>. Lagos: Federal Ministry of Information, 1969. 15 p.
Dr. Azikiwe renounces his support of Biafra on August 2 8, 1969 and declares his complete support for a strong united Nigeria.

Ballard, J. A. "Administrative origins of Nigerian federalism," <u>African Affairs</u>, LXX (Oct. 1971), 333-48.

Balogun, Ola. "Le Dossier fédéral: la question de l'auto-détermination et la guerre civile au Nigéria," <u>Rev. Fr. Etud. Pol. Afr.</u>, (Jan. 1970), 40-3.

Booth, A. R. "Two levels of truth: the case for Nigeria," <u>Help</u>, (April 1969), 28-30.

Brand, J. A. "The Mid-West State Movement in Nigerian politics: a study in formation," <u>Pol. Stud.</u>, XIII (Oct. 1965), 346-65.

Brett, Lionel, ed. <u>Constitutional problems of federalism in Nigeria</u>. Lagos: Times Press, 1961. 247 p.
Proceedings of a seminar held at King's College, Lagos, 8-15 August 1960, under the auspices of the Ford Foundation of America, edited by a Judge of Nigerian Supreme Court. Appendix contains two background papers on the historical evolution of the Federation, specifying the Legislative and Executive powers as well as fundamental rights.

Bruce, J. W. "The Creation of the Mid-West region and its significance for Nigerian federalism." In Andrew Cordier, ed. <u>Columbia essays in international affairs</u>:

(FEDERALISM, CONFEDERALISM AND MINORITY PROBLEMS)

the Dean's papers. New York: Columbia University, 1967, pp. 111-39.

Carol, Hans. "The Making of Nigeria's political regions," J. Asian Afr. Stud., III (July 1968), 271-86.

"The Case for Nigeria," Nigerian Opinion, (Aug. 1967), 230-2.

Churchill, Winston. "Can the Nigerian crisis have a military solution?" Times (London), March 6, 1969, p. 8.
In the last of the series of his articles on the war, the author examines the case for preserving the Federation, the miscalculations of both the Federal and Biafran leadership, foreign interests and relief operations. Concludes that the maintenance of the Federation is in the economic interest of Britain and Nigeria and that "the general principle of maintaining existing African states as they are and discouraging the further Balkanization of Africa is sound. Africa is too large; tribal units too small."

Citizens' Committee for Independence. The Case for more states; memorandum submitted to the Minorities Commission. Lagos, 1957. 61 p. (Publication No. 2.)
The report of the Willink Commission appointed by the British Government to inquire into the minority problems in Nigeria was issued in 1958.

Cole, R. T. "Universities and federalism in post-civil war Nigeria," South Atlantic Q., LXX (Autumn 1970), 449-66.

"Creating the states," West Africa, No. 2635 (1967), 1537; No. 2636 (1967), 1569; No. 2637 (1967), 1603.

Davidson, Basil. "Which way Nigeria? 1. Towards a new Federation." West Africa, No. 2757 (April 11, 1970), 385.
Despite the bitterness of both sides in the conflict, a new Nigeria will eventually emerge

_____ "Which way Nigeria? 2. Towards a new society." West Africa, No. 2785 (April 18, 1970), 430-1.
"The immediate objective should be: consolidation of the military victory, rehabilitation of displaced persons throughout the Federation, and reconstruction of essential services."

(FEDERALISM, CONFEDERALISM AND MINORITY PROBLEMS)


"Difficult choice: conflict between tribalism and nationalism," Newsweek, LXXIV
(Nov. 3, 1969), 52-3.
Describes the military situation, the defection of Azikiwe to the Federal side and
observes that "the countries of Africa must make a difficult, but inescapable,
choice - either to strengthen national loyalties by creating societies in which the
component tribes co-exist or face the prospect that their borders may have to be
redrawn."


Dudley, Billy J. "The Concepts of federalism," Nigerian J. Econ. Soc. Stud.,
V (March 1963), 95-103.


_____ "Federalism and the balance of political power in Nigeria," J. Commonwealth
Pol. Stud., IV (March 1966), 16-29.
Critical examination of the application of federalism to Nigeria.


Ekpenyong, E. U. "Nigeria, Biafra and the South-Eastern State," Cont. Rev.,
CCXIII (Aug. 1968), 62-6.


Eleazu, Uma Oku. "Federalism and nation-building in Nigeria: a study of political
integration in a plural society," Doctoral Dissertation, University of California,
Los Angeles, 1969. 338 p.


Elias, Taslim Olawale. Federation vs. confederation and Nigerian federation. Port
of Spain: Office of the Premier of Trinidad and Tobago, 1960. 50 p.
Dr. Elias, Nigeria's Attorney-General for many years, is the current Chief Justice
of the Federation.
_____ Government and politics in Africa. 2n ed. New York: Asia Publishing House,
1963. 228 p.
A written version of the series of public lectures the author gave summer and
autumn of 1956 as Visiting Professor of Political Science, University of Delhi, India.


"The End of Regions," West Africa, No. 2610 (June 10, 1967), 746-7.
The political significance of the Federal decree of May 27, 1967, dividing the four
Regions of Nigeria into twelve states.

(FEDERALSIM, CONFEDERALISM AND MINORITY PROBLEMS)

Eyoma, E. I.   The Question of the minorities.  Stockholm: the Tanzanian Embassy, 1969.  5 p. (mimeographed).
The political significance of the loyalty of the minority tribes in former Biafra; both sides claimed it.

Ezera, Kalu.  "The Failure of Nigerian federalism and proposed constitutional changes," Africa Forum, (Summer 1966),  17-30.
Dr. Ezera, an outspoken Ibo scholar, a former Professor of Political Science at the University of Nigeria, and Member of Nigerian Parliament, died immediately after the civil war.

_____   Federalism and the quest for national unity in Africa with particular reference to Nigeria; contribution to the 6th World Congress, Geneva, September 21-25, 1964. Paris: International Political Science Association, 1964.  24 p.

"La Faillité de la Fédération du Nigéria," Rev. Fr. Etud. Pol. Afr., (June 1968), 47-64.

Friedrich, C. J.  Trends of federalism in theory and practice.  London: Pall Mall Press, 1969.

Gavin, R. J.  "History and political integration," Nigerian Opinion,  (Dec. 1967), 274-9; (Feb. 1968),  290-3.

Glickman, Harvey.  "Regionalism and micro-politics: dialogues on the theory of African political development, Part II," Africa Report, XII (June 1967),  31-2.

Great Britain.  Colonial Office.   Report of the Commission appointed to inquire into the fears of minorities and the means of allaying them.  London: H. M. S. O. , 1958. (Cmnd. 505.)
Chairman: Sir Henry Willink.

Ibo State Union.  The Ibo State Union memorandum to the Willink Minorities Commission, including addresses of the counsels at Calabar and Port Harcourt and the important events in the making of the history of Ibo land, 1841-1958, including Ibo land distance mileage charts.  Port Harcourt: Nigerian Popular Printing Press and Bookshop, 1958.  38 p.

(FEDERALISM, CONFEDERALISM AND MINORITY PROBLEMS)


Jakande, Latif Kayode. The Case for a Lagos state. Lagos: John West Publications, 1966. 36 p.
Lagos, the federal capital of Nigeria, was made a separate state by the Constitutional Decree of May 27, 1967.

Legality of the Government of Nigeria. Enugu: Govt. Printer, 1967. 4 p.
Rejects the government that superseded the Ironsi regime as the legal government.

Legum, Colin. "When two rights conflict," Observer (London), March 16, 1969, p. 8.
The Federal case for a strong united Nigeria and the Biafran claim to right of self-determination.


Mackintosh, John P. "The Nigerian Federal Parliament," Public Law, (Autumn 1963), 333-61.


MacLaughlin, D. B. and M. Hazen. "Federal and Regional roles in Nigeria," Seminar Paper, Institute of Commonwealth Studies, London, 1968 (mimeographed).


Matthews, R. O. "Domestic and inter-state conflict in Africa," Int. Journal (Summer 1970), 459-85.


Mayo-Smith, I. "A New administrative structure for the new states," Administration (Ibadan), (April 1968), 169-79.


Meisler, Stanley. "North still a puzzle in Nigerian equation; strong elements of separatism remains despite its support of the Federal Government," L.A. Times, Sept. 15, 1969, Part 1, p. 18.
Provides good background information on the war, examining the historical, cultural and economic factors in the outbreak of the conflict, with special attention to Northern Nigeria.


"Les Minorités font la loi," Jeune Afrique, No. 404, (Oct. 6, 1968), 22-3.


Nigeria. Federal Ministry of Information. Birth of new Nigeria. Lagos, 1967. 24 p.
An important publication giving the text of the broadcast to the nation by General Gowon, Head of the Nigerian Military Government, on May 27, 1967, announcing

48

(FEDERALISM, CONFEDERALISM AND MINORITY PROBLEMS)

the division of Nigerian Regions into twelve states.


_____ Nigeria, 12 state-structure, the only way out. Lagos, 1968. 21 p.
Contends that the political stability of Nigeria rests on implementation of the State
Decree of May 27, 1967.
Nigeria, Western State. Ministry of Home Affairs and Information. Guide to new
administrative units in Western Nigeria. Ibadan, 1967. 15 p.


"Nigerian war: Biafra's claim to constitutional legitimacy," Times (London), March
6, 1969, p. 9.
Letters to the editor with opposing viewpoints.


Nwabueze, Benjamin O. Reflections on the review of the Nigerian constitution.
Lagos: Times Press, 1963. 31 p.
Dr. Nwabueze is Professor of Law at the University of Lagos.

Nwankwo, Arthur. Nigeria: the challenge of Biafra. London: Rex Collings, 1973.
The author is co-author of Biafra: the making of a nation (1969) and a joint
publisher of Nwankwo-Ifejika & Co., one of the most promising Nigerian indigenous
publishers.


Nwanze, M. C. "Co-operation and tension in Nigerian federalism," Leeds African
Studies Bulletin, (Oct. 1967), 11-12.


Nziramasanga, M. "Secession, federalism, and African unity," In Joseph Okpaku,
ed. Nigeria, dilemma of nationhood. New York: Third Press, 1972, pp. 229-57.


O'Connell, James. "Political integration: the Nigerian case."
In Arthur Hazlewood, ed. African integration and disintegration: case studies in
economic and political union. London: Oxford University Press, 1967, pp. 129-84.


_____ "The Politics of majorities and minorities," Nigerian Opinion, III, No. 7
(1967), 216-9.


Odenigwe, Godwin A. "The Constitutional development of Nigeria: the origins of

(FEDERALISM, CONFEDERALISM AND MINORITY PROBLEMS)


federalism, 1862-1954," Doctoral Dissertation, Clark University (U.S.), 1957.


Odumosu, Oluwole Idowu. The Nigerian constitution: history and development.
London: Sweet & Maxwell, 1963. 407 p. (Law in Africa, No. 4.)
Constitutional history of Nigeria from the British annexation of Lagos in 1861 to
independence in 1960. Includes text of Nigerian constitution.


Ogunsheye, Ayo. "Problem of federation in Africa," In H. Passin and K. A. B.
Jones-Quartey, eds. Africa: the dynamics of change. Ibadan: Ibadan University
Press, 1963, pp. 89-107.


Ogwurike, C. O. "Aims of Nigerian federalism," Nigerian Law J., I (Dec. 1965),
194+.


_____ "The Federation of Nigeria (its federal aspects and federal constitution),"
Doctoral Dissertation, London University, 1962.


Okere, T. "La Fédération du Nigéria: un défi," Tam-Tam, (Feb. 1969), 27-30.


Ola, O. "Nigeria: the limits of confederalism," J. Business Soc. Stud., I
(Sept. 1968), 89-95.


Onipede, F. Oladipe. "Nigerian crisis; legality and legitimacy of the January coup,"
Africa Quarterly, IX, No. 3 (1969), 233-50.


Onwu, Chukwu A. "Nigeria at the crossroads," New African, (March 1967), 5-6.


Otegbeye, Tunji. "Nigeria and the national question," Peace, Freedom and Socialism. (London), (Oct. 1969), 24-6.


Otubushin, Ch. O. Nigeria's hour of decision. Yaba, Nigeria: Pacific Printers,
1967. 15 p.

(FEDERALISM, CONFEDERALISM AND MINORITY PROBLEMS)

Pace, Eric. "Biafra's Ibo leaders strive to insure the continued support of minority tribes," N.Y. Times, Sept. 14, 1969, p. 12.
The loyalty of the people from the minority areas in Biafra was claimed by both the Biafran and Federal Governments.

"Preserving unity by staying apart," Time, LXXXIX (Jan. 27, 1967), 36.
During the Aburi meeting in Ghana in January 1967, the Military Governor of Eastern Nigeria, Odumegwu Ojukwu, argued that in the light of rioting and killings of Ibos in Northern Nigeria and general political confusion, it might be more prudent for the Regions to stay apart (giving each absolute autonomy) until temper had cooled and thus preserve the integrity of the country than continue in the confused situation capable of exploding into disintegration of Nigeria.

"The Primacy of security: an Eastern viewpoint," Nigerian Opinion, III, Nos. 5-6 (1967), 203.

Problems of Nigerian minorities; being independent commentary on the proceedings of Sir Henry Willink Commission of Inquiry into the fears of Nigerian minorities and on the general set-up of Nigerian politics. Lagos: Pacific Printing Workd, 1958? 34 p.
Divided into three parts: Western Nigeria, Eastern Nigeria and Northern Nigeria, it reviews the recommendations of the Commission and the arguments or complaints of representatives at the inquiry.

"Real issues at Lagos conference (1966)," Nigerian Opinion, II, No. 10 (1966), 112-4.
All-Nigeria Ad Hoc Constitutional Conference in September 1966, ended without results.

Rothchild, Donald S. "The Limits of federalism; an examination of political institutional transfer in Africa," J. Mod. Afr. Stud., IV (Nov. 1966), 275-93.
Reviews the application of federal structure to various African countries, including Nigeria, indicating its strengths and weaknesses. Dr. Rothchild is Professor of Political Science, University of California, Davis.

_____ "New trends in African integration," Africa Today, XV (Nov./Dec. 1968), 6-8.

# Nigerian Civil War: An Annotated Bibliography

(FEDERALISM, CONFEDERALISM AND MINORITY PROBLEMS)

Rothchild, Donald S. "Safeguarding Nigeria's minorities; the appeal of formation of separate states," Duquesne Review, VIII (Spring 1963), 35-51.

_____ Toward unity in Africa: a study of federalism in British Africa. With a foreword by Gwendolen Carter. Washington, D.C., Public Affairs Press, 1960. 224 p. Rev: Amer. Hist. Rev., LXVII (Oct. 1961), 215.

Schröder, D. "Die Bundesstaatlichkeit in Nigeria," Verfassung und Recht in Ubersee, I, No. 1 (1968), 30-42.

Smith, J. H. "The Creation of state administrations in former Northern Region of Nigeria," Administration (Ibadan) (April 1968), 121-9.

Stephens, Robert. "A Voice for minorities," Observer (London), Nov. 30, 1969, p. 8. Examines minority problems in Europe, Asia, and Africa, with special reference to the Nigerian Civil War.

Tamuno, Tekena N. "Patriotism and statism in the Rivers State," African Affairs, LXXI (July 1972), 264-81.

Tickle, I. "Twelve states in Nigeria," Legon Observer, III, No. 10 (1968), 2-3. Although he welcomes the 12 state-structure, the author argues that it might be construed as a means of destroying the secessionist state.
Towards a new Nigeria. Lagos: African Statesman, 1970. 20 p. (African Statesman supplement, No. 2.)

"Towards one Nigeria," Nigerian Opinion, II, No. 4 (1966), 1-2.

Vickers, M. "Establishment and maintenance of Centre rule in modern Nigeria," Africa Quarterly, VIII, No. 4 (1969), 327-42.

Wali, Obi. "An Experience in Rivers State of Nigeria," Pan African J., III, No. 2 (1970), 66-70.

(FEDERALISM, CONFEDERALISM AND MINORITY PROBLEMS)


"Who are the confederalists," <u>Nigerian Opinion,</u> III, No. 2 (1967), 158-9.


Zanzolo, Albert. "The National question and Nigeria," <u>African Communist,</u> XXXVI (1969), 18-24.


Zolberg, Aristide. <u>Creating political order: the party states of West Africa.</u>
Chicago: Rand McNally, 1966. 168 p. (Studies in political change.)
Rev: <u>World Politics,</u> XX (Oct. 1967), 128.


_____ "Patterns of national integration," <u>J. Mod. Afr. Stud.</u>, V (Dec. 1967), 449-67.


_____ "Structure of political conflict in the new states of tropical Africa," <u>Amer. Pol. Sci. Rev.</u>, LXII (March 1968), 70-87.

## BIAFRA, NIGERIAN AND AFRICAN UNITY

Achebe, Chinua. "The African writer and the Biafran cause," Conch, I (March 1969), 8-14.
The author, a celebrated Ibo novelist, is currently Senior Research Fellow in the Institute of African Studies, University of Nigeria.


_____ Christmas in Biafra and other stories. New York: Doubleday, 1973.


_____ Gods at war and other stories. New York: Doubleday, 1973.


_____ et al. The Insider: stories of war and peace from Nigeria. Enugu: Nwankwo-Ifejika & Co., 1971. 130 p.
An anthology of short stories by writers with an inside knowledge of Nigerian social and political problems. The writers include Chinua Achebe, Arthur Nwankwo and Samuel Ifejika who are both publishers of the Nwankwo-Ifejika & Co. and authors of The Making of a Nation: Biafra (1969), and Flora Nwapa, first Nigerian woman novelist.


Aligwekwe, A. "Biafra: reflections on the nation state in Sub-Saharan Africa," Insight and Opinion, (Accra), III, No. 2 (1968), 41-53.


Arikpo, Okoi. A Testimony of faith; being the full text of the statement by Dr. Okoi Arikpo, the Nigerian Commissioner for External Affairs at the Twenty-third Session of the General Assembly of the United Nations on October 11, 1968. Apapa: Nigerian National Press, 1968? 13 p.
The anthropologist reiterates the position of the Federal Government in the war and its persistent efforts to find a political solution provided that the secessionists renounce their independence and accept the reunification of the country.


Asika, Anthony Ukpabi. Reflections on the political evolution of one Nigeria. Enugu: Administrator's Office, 1969.


Asuhoa, R. I. Pourquoi le Biafra? Paris: Editions du Sapin d'Or, 1969. 169 p.


Atemengue, J. Nigéria concilier l'inconciliable. Paris: La Gazette Africaine et

(BIAFRA, NIGERIAN AND AFRICAN UNITY)

Malgache, Les Cahiers d'Afrique, 1968. **64** p. (mimeographed).

Atemengue, J. Pourquoi le Nigéria? Paris: La Gazette Africaine et Malgache, Les Cahiers de l'Afrique, 1968. 54 p. (mimeographed).

Azuonye, et al. Gedichte aus Biafra. Berlin: Hermann Luchterhand Verlag, 1969. unpaged.

Baker, Ross. "The Emergence of Biafra: Balkanization or nation-building?" Orbis, XII (Summer 1968), 518-33.
Examines the impact of the survival of Biafra as an independent nation on African unity.

Bakole, M. M. "The African unity, today and tomorrow." Présence Africaine, No. 53 (Jan. 1965), 147-58.

Balogun, O. "La Question d'auto-détermination et guerre civile au Nigéria," Rev. Fr. Etud. Pol. Afr., No. 49 (Jan. 1970), 40-3.

Barrett, Lindsay. "The Nigerian crisis: an arena for Africa's struggle for self-determination," Negro Digest, XVIII (Oct. 1969), 10-15.

Bassey, L. A. "Is Biafra viable?" Pan-African J., III (Winter 1969), 10-14.

Beaumont, Jacques. "Unité du Nigéria, unité africaine," Christianisme Social (Paris), Nos. 1-2 (1969), 45-6.

Beijbom, A. et al. Raport fran Biafra. Stockholm: A. B. Tryckmans, 1968. 107 p.

Biafra. Ministry of Information. Biafra deserves world sympathy. Enugu, 1968? 8 p.
Rejects the view that the Federal Government is the only legal Government in

(BIAFRA, NIGERIAN AND AFRICAN UNITY)

Nigeria and appeals to the world to support Biafra.


"Biafra explains its case," Washington Post, April 21, 1969, p. A13.
The Biafran case put before the American people by the Biafran envoy. Explains Biafra's opposition to the relief plans made by some relief agencies and countries, and attacks the Soviet support of the Federal Government, while suggesting that the United States, being the only Big Power not directly involved in the conflict, initiate peace efforts towards an equitable political settlement.


"Le Biafra: histoire d'une sécession; naissance d'une nation," Rev. Def. Nat., XXV (March 1969), 414.


"Biafra: nearing the third year," Times (London), April 28, 1969, p. 9.
An editorial calling for a political settlement of the war, as Biafra hangs on despite loss of most of its territory.


"Biafran tragedy," Nation, CCX (Jan. 26, 1970), 66-7.


Bipoun-Woum, Joseph-Marie. Le Droit international africain: problèmes généraux - règlement de conflit. Paris: Librairie Générale de Droit et de Jurisprudence, 1970. 327 p. (Bibliothèque africaine et malgache, droit et sociologie politique, Vol. V.)


Bohannan, Paul, ed. Law and warfare: studies in anthropology of conflict. Garden City, New York: Natural History Press for the American Museum of Natural History, 1967. 441 p. (American Museum source books in anthropology.) Examination of the two basic forms of conflict resolution.
Rev: Amer. Anthrop., LXX (June 1968), 579.


Bolea, F. de. "La Sécession de Biafra," Africa (Madrid), No. 309 (1967), 29.


Boutros-Ghali, Boutros. L'Organisation de l'Unité Africaine. Paris: A. Colin, 1968. 197 p.

(BIAFRA, NIGERIAN AND AFRICAN UNITY)

Bühler, Jean. Biafra-Tragödie eines begabten Volkes. Zurick-Stuttgart: Flamberg
Verlag, 1968. 169 p.


"The Case for Nigeria," Nigerian Opinion (Aug. 1967), 230-2.


Cavanagh, M. "Tragedy and farce in Nigeria," Tablet, CCXXII (March 23, 1968),
277-8.


"Challenge of Biafra," Commonweal, XC (July 25, 1969), 451-2.


Chegwe, A. O. Biafra-Tragödie eines Volkes. Wiesbaden: Selbstverlag, 1969. 92 p.


"Chinua Achebe on Biafra," Transition, VII, No. 36 (1968), 31-8.
An interview.


Clinton, J. V. "The Ibo rebels," Cont. Rev., CCXIII, No. 1231 (1968), 57-61.


Cornevin, Robert. "Y a-t-il une nation biafraise?" Dire (Geneva) (Feb. 1970), 36-42.


_____ "Ibo et non-Ibo; les chances d'une nation biafraise," Rev. Psych. Peuples
(Autumn 1969), 157-67.


Crowther, C. Edward. "The Agony of Biafra." Episcopalian (March 1969), 11-13.
An eye-witness account of the situation in Biafra by Episcopal Assistant Bishop of
California in the United States.


Cruise O'Brien, Conor. "Inside Biafra," Observer (London), Oct. 8, 1967, p. 9.


Debré, François. "Le Conflit nigéro-biafrais: première guerre nationale africaine,"
Rev. Fr. Etud. Pol. Afr. (March 1969), 29-47.

# *Nigerian Civil War: An Annotated Bibliography*

(BIAFRA, NIGERIAN AND AFRICAN UNITY)

Decreane, Philippe.    "Nigéria: les chances de Biafra," <u>Mois en Afrique</u>, (June 1967),  20-2.


_____ "Nigéria: la solution finale du problème biafrais," <u>Rev. Fr. Etud. Pol. Afr.</u>, No. 33  (Sept. 1968),  2-4..


_____ "Nigéria: sécession à l'état," <u>Mois en Afrique</u>,  No. 17  (1967),  8-11.


Diamond, Stanley.  "The Biafran possibility," <u>Africa Report</u>,  XIII  (Feb. 1968),  16-19. Justifies the secession, emphasizing the economic and political viability of Biafra.


_____ "Une Ethnocide," <u>Les Temps Modernes</u>  (Feb. 1970),  1194-1206.


_____ "Reflections on the African revolution: the point of the Biafran case," <u>J. Asian Afr. Stud.</u>,  V  (Jan/Apr. 1970),  16-28.


_____ "Who killed Biafra?" <u>N.Y. Rev. Bks.</u>  (Feb. 26, 1970),  17-27.


Dienne, M.  "Nigerian patriots want national unity," <u>World Marxist Review</u>, (Toronto) (Oct. 1967),  16-19.


Dudley, Billy J.  "Eastern Nigeria goes it alone: the drift towards open conflict," <u>Round Table</u>,  LVII  (July 1967),  318-24. The secession of Eastern Nigeria on May 30, 1967, made war inevitable.


"An End to a journey and an end to flight," <u>Newsweek</u>,  LXXIII (March 24, 1969),  55. News conference with the Biafran leader, C. Odumegwu Ojukwu.


Esedebe, P. O.  "Why international opinion supports Biafra," <u>Legon Observer</u>,  IV, No. 16  (1969),  9-10.

(BIAFRA, NIGERIAN AND AFRICAN UNITY)

Forsyth, Frederick. "Will the world let Biafra survive?" Illus. Lond. News. (Jan. 3, 1970), 12-13.


Gache, P. "Les Noirs ne se mélangent pas," Spectacle du Monde (Paris), LXXIV (May 1968), 67-73.
Racial hatred in Africa illustrated by the Nigerian war.


Garrison, Lloyd. "Biafra versus Nigeria; the other dirty little war," N.Y. Times Magazine (March 31, 1968), 36-47; 50-4.


_____ "Ibos go it alone," N.Y. Times Magazine (June 19, 1967), 746-7.
The secession of May 30, 1967.


_____ "Odumegwu Ojukwu is Biafra," N.Y. Times Magazine (June 22, 1969), 7-9+.


"General Gowon talks to the editor," West Africa, No. 2673 (Aug. 24, 1968), 971-2.


Gentili, A. M. "Biafra un occasione per ripensare l'Africa," Il Mulino (April 1969), 370-81.


Gold, Herbert. "My summer vacation in Biafra," Harper's Magazine, CCXXXIX (Nov. 1969), 63-8.
Experiences of the American novelist in Biafra.


Gowon, Yakubu. Long live African unity; address by Major-General Yakubu Gowon at the Assembly of Heads of States of the Organization of African Unity at Addis Ababa on Sept. 6, 1969. Lagos: Nigerian National Press, 1969. 8 p.


Graham-Douglas, Nabo B. Ojukwu's rebellion and world opinion. Apapa, Nigeria: Nigerian National Press, 1968? 24 p.
The author, a noted Nigerian lawyer from the Rivers State and former Attorney-General for Eastern Nigeria, is currently Federal Attorney-General.

# Nigerian Civil War: An Annotated Bibliography

(BIAFRA, NIGERIAN AND AFRICAN UNITY)

Green, Reginald and Ann Seidman. Unity or poverty? The economics of Pan-
Africanism. With a foreword by Thomas Hodgkin. Harmondsworth: Penguin, 1968.
364 p. (Penguin African library, AP.23.)

Hadj-Chinkh, B. "Les Promoteurs de la sécession du Nigéria," Rev. Pol. Int.,
XIX, No. 432 (1968), 23-4.

Hanisch, R. Burgerkrieg in Afrika? Biafra und die inneren Konflikte eines
Kontinents. Berlin: Colloquium Verlag, 1970. 78 p.

Hatch, John. "Why secession would be disastrous for black Africa," New Statesman,
LXXIX (Jan. 9, 1970), 40-3.

Himmelstrand, Ulf. "Tribalism, nationalism, rank-equilibration and social structure;
a theoretical interpretation of some socio-political processes in Southern Nigeria,"
J. Peace Res., No. 2 (1969), 81-103.
Concludes that "the creation of a larger number of ethnically fairly homogeneous
but economically not viable and politically not very powerful states within a federal
structure will help to break up the power of threatening regional particularism and
to emphasize interpendence within the national economy. This in turn will facilitate
the emergence of less vulnerable national organization of functional interests, such
as trade unions, that will constitute the breeding ground for more universalistic
orientations among citizens."

Hegdepetti, William. "Biafra," Look, XXXIII (April 1, 1969), 22-8.

Howe, Russell Warren. "Nigeria at war," Edit. Res. Rpts., I (Feb. 28, 1968),
143-60.
Progress of war to preserve Nigerian unity; regional antagonisms; foreign interests.

Hutschenreuter, K. "Die Inneren Auseinandersetzungen in Nigeria um die Gestaltung
des Staatsaufbaus- Sezession oder Integration, Unitarismus oder Föderalismus,"
Asien, Afrika, Lateinamerika (Leipzig), (1968), 371-400.

(BIAFRA, NIGERIAN AND AFRICAN UNITY)

"Ibo ex-leader ends support of Biafra," <u>N.Y. Times</u>, Aug. 29, 1969, p. 2.
Dr. Nnamdi Azikiwe, former President of Nigeria.

"The Ibo in charge," <u>West Africa</u>, No. 2746 (Jan. 17, 1970), 65.
Anthony Asika, Administrator of the East Central State.

Ijalaye, D. A. "Some legal implications of the Nigerian Civil War," <u>Proceedings of</u>
<u>the First Annual Conference of the Nigerian Society of International Law.</u> Lagos,
1969, pp. 70-114.

_____ "Was Biafra at any time a state in international law?" <u>Amer. J. Int. Law,</u>
LXV (July 1971), 551-9.

Ikoku, S. G. "La Sécession biafraise: mythes et réalités," <u>Rev. Fr. Etud. Pol.</u>
<u>Afr.</u> (Jan. 1970), 56-64.

"Interview with General Gowon," <u>Time</u>, XCIV (July 4, 1969), 32.
Indicates Gowon's war policy and attitude towards the Ibos.

"An Interview with General Gowon," <u>West Africa</u>, No. 2712 (May 24, 1969), 574-5.

Jahn, Janheinz. "Die Auseinandersetzung um Biafra. Ihr Ablauf und ihre Hintergrunde," <u>Frankfurter Hefte</u>, No. 11 (Jan. 23, 1968), 756-66.

Jervis, Steven. "Nigeria and Biafra," <u>Africa Today</u>, XIV, No. 6 (1967), 16-18.

Kirk-Greene, A. H. M. "Nigeria can survive and still be one country," <u>Commonwealth</u>
<u>J.</u> (Feb. 1967), 3-10; 49-50.

_____ and C. C. Wrigley. "Biafra in print," <u>African Affairs</u>, LXIX (April 1970),
180-3.

(BIAFRA, NIGERIAN AND AFRICAN UNITY)

Knapp, G. <u>Aspects of the Biafran affair.</u> London: Biafran Association, 1969. 56 p.

Kooymans, P. M. "Biafra en het volkenrecht," <u>Kroniek van Africa</u> (1968), 26-31.

Kreker, Hans-Justus. "Nigerias Burgerkrieg - eine afrikanische Tragödie,"
    Wehrkunde (München), No. 8 (Jan. 17, 1968), 412-4.

Kudryavtsen, V. "Observer's opinion: blow to separatism," <u>Curr. Dig. Soviet Pr.</u>,
    XXII (Feb. 17, 1970), 14-15. Translated from <u>Izvestia</u>, Jan. 22, 1970.
    The fall of Biafra.

_____ "Problems and judgments; test of Africa's maturity," <u>Curr. Dig. Soviet Pr.</u>,
    XX (Oct. 30, 1968), 20-1.
    Condensed from <u>Izvestia</u>, Oct. 11, 1968, p. 2, it examines the war situation in its
    15th month duration and accuses the Western powers of imperialist design to
    destroy the Nigerian unity by engineering the secession.

Kyle, Keith. "The Significance of Biafra," <u>Listener</u>, LXXXIII (Jan. 22, 1970),
    103-4.

Laptev, V. "From Katanga to Biafra," <u>New Times</u> (Moscow), No. 52 (1967), 17-18.
    A gruelling civil war broke out in Zaire (former Belgian Congo) in 1960-61 when
    Katanga, an oil-rich province of that country, seceded from the Central Government
    owing to political and tribal differences. The secession was crushed only on the
    intervention of the United Nations.

Leapman, Michael. "Moral of Biafra's survival," <u>New Statesman</u>, LXXVII (March
    7, 1969), 317.

Legum, Colin. "Nationalism impact on Pan-Africanism," <u>East Africa Journal</u>, II
    (April 1965), 5-16; 38-40.

_____ "Nigeria versus Biafra; in taking sides," <u>Christianity and Crisis</u>," XXIX

(BIAFRA, NIGERIAN AND AFRICAN UNITY)


(May 26, 1969), 150-4.


"Life in what is 'Biafra': an Ibo view," Newsweek, LXXVI (July 20, 1970), 37.
Life in former Biafra seven months after the war.


Listowel, J. "Recovering from the Ibos," Tablet, CCXXIII (March 22, 1969), 290-1.


Mafo, Adeola. "The Ojukwu phenomenon," Nigerian Opinion, (March 1967), 173-5.


Manigat, M. "L'Organisation de l'Unité Africaine," Rev. Fr. Sci. Pol., XXI
(April 1971), 382-401.


Mazrui, Ali. The Trial of Christopher Okigbo. New York: The Third Press, 1972.
145 p.
A work of fiction in a dramatized setting in which the famous Nigerian poet is put
on trial for subordinating the principles of Nigerian unity and writing poetry to the
ideals of Biafran independence. Okigbo, a brilliant poet and Field Representative
of Cambridge University Press, was killed while fighting for Biafra. Dr. Mazrui
is Professor and Head of the Dept. of Political Science and Public Administration,
Makerere University, Uganda.
Rev: Library J., XCVII (Aug. 1972), 2646.
    N.Y. Times Bk. Rev., (Sept. 17, 1972), 48.
    Nation, CCXV (Aug. 21, 1972), 120.


Meisler, Stanley. "Biafra: war of images," Nation, CCVIII (March 10, 1969), 301-4.
Examines the effective use of propaganda by both sides.


_____ "Report: Nigeria and Biafra," Atlantic Monthly, CCXXIV (Oct. 1969), 25-6.


_____ "Tribalism and politics in Nigeria," World Today, XXII (Nov. 1966), 460-7.


Mezu, Sebastian O. "Du Nigéria oriental à la république du Biafra," Esprit (Paris)
(Dec. 1969), 787-806.

(BIAFRA, NIGERIAN AND AFRICAN UNITY)

"Mid-West invasion. Winning the war and the peace. Tragic illusions. The case for Nigeria," Nigerian Opinion, III, Nos. 8-9 (1967), 227-30.

"New phase in Biafra-O. A. U. relations," Legon Observer, III, No. 11 (1968), 1-2. While "recognizing a secessionist state is by definition a violation of major principle" ⌐of O. A. U.⌐, Presidents of Zambia and Tanzania take a different view in the Biafran context.

Nigeria. Federal Ministry of Information. Challenge of unity. Lagos, 1967.

_____ Ibos in a united Nigeria. Lagos, 1968. 8 p.
Attempts to correct the prevailing impression abroad that the Ibos would be subjected to servitude if they gave up secession. "They will live with their compatriots again in the peace and prosperity which served Nigeria so well for over half a century - the peace and prosperity in which the Ibos themselves thrived magnificently in leading positions in business, education, the professions and the public services. "

_____ Nigeria, the dream empire of a rebel? Lagos, 1967. 12 p.
Contends that the Biafran leader, Odumegwu Ojukwu, was filled with an inordinate desire for power in leading the Ibos to secession.

_____ Nigeria's struggle for survival; statement at a press conference in the Connaught Rooms, Kingsway, London, on Monday, July 17, 1967, by Chief Anthony Enahoro, Nigerian Federal Commissioner for Information and Labour. Lagos, 1967. 11 p.
The need to crush the secession and preserve national territorial integrity.

_____ The Struggle for one Nigeria. Lagos, 1967. 59 p.

_____ Towards one Nigeria, Nos. 1-3. Lagos, 1967.
Text of official news talks over Radio Nigeria, outlining Federal efforts to preserve Nigerian unity and territorial integrity.

_____ Unity in diversity. Lagos, 1967. 15 p.

(BIAFRA, NIGERIAN AND AFRICAN UNITY)

Nigeria, Mid-Western State. <u>Understanding the Nigerian crisis</u>. Benin City, 1968. 34 p.

Nigeria, Northern. Ministry of Information. <u>Nigeria, the realities of our time</u>. Kaduna, 1967. 25 p.

"Nigeria - Biafra unyielding," <u>Afr. Res. Bull</u>., V, No. 9 (1968), 1185-91.

"Nigeria - developments following secession," <u>Afr. Res. Bull</u>., IV, No. 6 (1967), 796-8.

"Nigeria - Eastern Region secedes," <u>Afr. Res. Bull</u>., IV, No. 5 (1967), 776-80.

"Nigéria - la sécession de la région orientale," <u>Afrique Contemporaine</u> (Paris), VI, No. 32 (1967), 21-2.

Nwafor, Azinna. "Born in fire: prelude to Biafra; the agony of independence and survival," <u>Michigan Q. Rev</u>., IX (April 1970), 93-103.

Nyerere, Julius. "On African unity," <u>Nigerian Opinion,</u> III, Nos. 5-6 (1967), 198-201. Dr. Nyerere was Tanzania's president when it became the first country to recognize Biafra on April 13, 1968. See <u>Africa Report</u>, XIII (June 1968), 27.

"O.A.U. and Nigeria," <u>West Africa</u>, No. 2659 (May 18, 1968), 565-6.

Ojukwu, Chukwuemeka Odumegwu. <u>Address...to the Joint Meeting of Advisory Committee of Chiefs and Elders and the Consultative Assembly, Friday, May 26, 1967</u>. Enugu: Govt. Printer, 1967. 34 p.
The most important and last address made by Ojukwu to this body before the secession. Given the mandate by this Assembly, on May 30, 1967, Eastern Nigeria was declared "Republic of Biafra." War was then unavoidable.

\_\_\_\_\_ "Text of the statement by General Ojukwu on the situation in defeated Biafra,"

(BIAFRA, NIGERIAN AND AFRICAN UNITY)

<u>N.Y. Times</u>, Jan. 16, 1970, p. 12.
The first formal statement by former Biafran leader purported to have been given in Switzerland after his flight from the collapsing state.


"Ojukwu has made his point," <u>Economist</u> (Aug. 30, 1969), 13.


Panter-Brick, S. K. "The Right of self-determination; its application to Nigeria," <u>Int. Affairs</u> (London), XLIV (April 1968), 254-66.


Parker, Franklin. "Biafra and the Nigerian Civil War," <u>Negro Hist. Bull.</u>, XXXII (Dec. 1969), 7-11.


Perham, Margery. "The Nigerian crisis and after," <u>Listener</u>, LXXV (Jan. 27, 1966), 121-3.


Plowman, E. E. "Anguish over Biafra," <u>Christianity Today</u>, XII (Aug. 30, 1968), 44-5.


Post, K. W. J. "Is there a case for Biafra?" <u>Int. Affairs</u> (London), XLIV (Jan. 1968), 26-39.


<u>Proclamation of the Republic of Biafra</u>. Enugu: Govt. Printer, 1967. 18 p.


"Proclamation of the Republic of Biafra," <u>Int. Legal Mat.</u> (Current documents) (July 1967), 665-80.
The legal and constitutional validity and implications of the secession on May 30, 1967.


"Propaganda for Biafra," <u>Tablet</u>, CCXXIII (Jan. 4, 1969), 3.


Rake, Alan. "Azikiwe: time for a come-back?" <u>Observer</u> (London), Aug. 31, 1969, p. 5.

(BIAFRA, NIGERIAN AND AFRICAN UNITY)

Dr. Azikiwe's renunciation of his support of Biafra and declaration of his faith in a strong re-united Nigeria on August 29, 1969.

"Reflections on the Nigerian revolution," South Atlantic Q., IV (1966), 421-30.

Reik, Miriam. "Biafra's unifying goal: an independent democratic black state," Christian Sci. Mon., Aug. 7, 1969, p. 9.
Assessment of Biafra's goals and political ideology by Professor of Literature at Temple University in the United States.

Renard, Alain. Biafra, naissance d'une nation? Paris: Aubier-Montaigne, 1969, 256 p. (Collection tiers-monde et développement.)
Rev: Conch, I (Sept. 1969), 63-4.

Renschler, R. "Biafra im Jahre 3." Liberal (Bonn), XI, No. 6 (1969), 450-7.

Schneyder, P. "Le Martyre du Biafra," Esprit (Oct. 1968), 414-9.

Shimony, Annemarie A. "The Biafran tragedy," In Donald R. Cutler, ed. The religious situation: 1969. Boston: Beacon Press, 1969, pp. 91-112.
Includes extensive bibliography.

Soyinka, Wole. The man died. London: Rex Collings, 1972. 224 p.
The hero of this book is Colonel Fajuyi, Military Governor of Western Nigeria, Jan. 17-July 29, 1966, who died along with Head of the Federal Military Government, General Aguiyi-Ironsi, on July 1966. Both coups of 1966 are discussed as well as the activities of Colonel Banjo, Yoruba, who was a traitor to both sides of the conflict. The author states, "If the original aims of January 15 [1966] had succeeded, I cannot honestly say that I would not have supported it all the way, although not as a perennial institution. Military intervention is not necessarily evil, but the suggestion that military rule is the answer is an insult to most of the progressive regimes in Africa today."
The author, a Yoruba, is the famous African playwright; he has also published poetry and fiction.

(BIAFRA, NIGERIAN AND AFRICAN UNITY)

"Special Biafra," Jeune Afrique, No. 473 (Jan. 27, 1970), 22-36.

"The State of the East," Nigerian Opinion, III, No. 2 (1967), 160-2.

Thompson, W. Scott and Richard Bisell. "Legitimacy and authority in the O.A.U,"
  Afr. Stud. Rev., XV (April 1972), 17-42.
  Critical study of the provisions, powers and limitations of the Organization of
  African Unity.

Thompson, Vincent Bakpetu. Africa and unity: the evolution of Pan-Africanism.
  With a foreword by Basil Davidson. London: Longmans, 1969. 412 p.
  A study of the efforts made by African leaders to achieve political and economic
  unity.
  Rev: African Affairs, LXX (Jan. 1971), 84-5.

"Towards unity through tribulation," Times (London), Sept. 30, 1970, p. 1.
  Preservation of Nigerian territorial integrity at a great cost of human lives and
  material devastation.

Toynbee, Arnold J. "Die Menschheit bezeugt noch immer nicht," Der Spiegel
  (Hamburg), No. 34 (Aug. 19, 1968), 77-80.
  Interview held by Der Spiegel with the British philosopher and historian on the war.

Van der Meullen, J. "Biafra en Afrika," Kroniek van Afrika (1968), 32-8.

Varma, S. N. "National unity and political stability in Nigeria," Int. Stud., IV
  (Jan. 1963), 265-80.

Vereiter, Karl von. Biafra. Translated from the German by E. Sanchez y Pacaul.
  Barcelona: Edit. Petronio, 1970. 189 p.

Vianney, J. "Gibt es in Afrika ein Recht auf Sezession?" Afrika Heute (Bonn), Nr.
  21 (1968), 313-5.

(BIAFRA, NIGERIAN AND AFRICAN UNITY)

Wallström, T. <u>Biafra</u>. Stockholm: Pan/Norstedts, 1968. 120 p.

Waugh, Auberon. "Hail Biafra," <u>Spectator</u>, (Aug. 2, 1968), 151-4.

Whiteman, Kaye. "Enugu: the psychology of secession." In S. K. Panter-Brick, ed. <u>Nigerian politics and military rule: prelude to the civil war</u>. London: Athlone Press, 1970, pp. 111-27.

Wodié, Francis. <u>La Sécession du Biafra et le droit international public</u>. Paris: Pedone, 1970. 44 p.

Wolpe, Howard E. "Port-Harcourt: a community of strangers: the politics of urban development in Eastern Nigeria," Doctoral Dissertation, Massachusetts Institute of Technology, 1967.
An oil-rich port, before the war predominantly peopled by the Ibos although located in non-Ibo area. Captured from the Biafran troops by the Federal forces on May 19, 1968, it has remained till today the Capital of the Rivers State, one of the three states carved out of the former Eastern Region.

Zieser, G. N. "Die Propagandastrategie Biafras im nigerianischen Burgerkrieg, 1967-1970; eine Modelle-Untersuchung zur interkulturellen Kommunikation zwischen Entwicklungs und Industrieländern," Phil. Diss., Salzburg, 1970, 223 p.
A study of the use of propaganda by both sides in the war, with special reference to its effective utilization by Biafra.

# Nigerian Civil War: An Annotated Bibliography

## THE MILITARY RULE - OBJECTIVES AND PROBLEMS

Adedeji, Adebayo. "The Men who keep Nigeria going," West Africa, No. 2753 (March 14, 1970), 281; No. 2756 (April 4, 1970), 363-5; No. 2757 (April 11, 1970), 396-7; No. 2758 (April 18, 1970), 433.

Akinyemi, A. Bolaji. "Nigeria: what should follow army rule - and when?" Africa Report, XVI (Feb. 1971), 22-3.
A critique of the Nigerian Military Government's decision to hand over power to the civilian government in 1976.

"The Armies of Africa," Africa Report, IX (Jan. 1964). Entire issue.
Country-by-country analysis of the armed forces of different African countries - their size, sources of external military assistance; defense pacts, etc.

"The Army, discipline and unity," Nigerian Opinion, II, No. 9 (1966), 100.

Baker, Pauline H. "The Politics of Nigerian military rule: the army plans phased reforms and transfer of power while conservative and socialist political factions wait," Africa Report, XVI (Feb. 1971), 18-21.

Baldus, B. "Zur gesellschaftlichen Funktion militarischer Gruppen in Afrika," In Paul Trappe, ed. Sozialer Wandel in Afrika südlich der Sahara. Hannover: Verlag für Literatur u. Zeitgeschehen, 1968.

Bell, M. J. V. Army and nation in sub-Saharan Africa. London: Institute for Strategic Studies, 1965. 16 p. (Adelphi papers, No. 21.)

_____ Military assistance to independent African states. London: Institute for Strategic Studies, 1964. (Adelphi papers, No. 15.)

Bienen, Henry. "Military assistance and political development," Paper presented at the International Sociological Association Meeting, London, Sept. 1967. 90 p.

_____, ed. The Military intervenes: case studies in political development. New York:

(THE MILITARY RULE - OBJECTIVES AND PROBLEMS)

Russell Sage Foundation, 1967. 175 p.

Brice, Belmont. "The Nature and the role of the military in sub-Saharan Africa," African Forum, II (Summer 1966), 57-67.

Broadcast to the nation, by His Excellency Major-General J. T. U. Aguiyi-Ironsi, Head of the National Military Government and Supreme Commander of the Armed Forces, the 24th of May, 1966. Lagos, 1966.
The most important but controversial decree promulgated by General Ironsi, which abolished political Regions and was aimed at unitary form of government. The opposition to this decree by Northern Nigeria resulted in the rioting in the area against the Ibos from May 30, 1966. This led to Ibo mass exodus to the East and to subsequent outbreak of the Civil War. By this decree, Nigeria ceased to be a Federation, becoming "simply the Republic of Nigeria...grouped into a number of territorial areas called provinces."

"Can the army remake Nigeria?" Economist (Jan. 29, 1966), 395-6.
The first military coup of Jan. 15, 1966, brought in the Ironsi regime which lasted only six months.

"Colonel Benjamin Adekunle - a Christian Yoruba," Afrique Actuelle (Paris), No. 33 (Nov. 1968), 35.

"Le Colonel Benjamin Adekunle parle," Jeune Afrique (Paris), No. 430 (April 6, 1969), 27-31.
An exclusive interview with Anette Léna of Jeune Afrique.

Crocker, Chester A. "Military and security problems in the international relations of Africa," Doctoral Dissertation, Johns Hopkins University, 1968?
Emphasis is on the historical development of the military forces in former British and French colonies in Africa and different methods used by Britain and France in transferring defense powers to those countries.

Cowan, Laing Gray. "The Military and African politics," International Journal (Toronto), XXI (Summer 1966), 289-97.

(THE MILITARY RULE - OBJECTIVES AND PROBLEMS)


Daalder, H. The Role of the military in the emerging countries. The Hague: Mouton, 1962. 25 p.


Dent, Martin J. "The Military and politics." In S. K. Panter-Brick, ed. Nigerian politics and military rule: prelude to the civil war. London: Athlone Press, 1970, pp. 78-93.


_____ "The Military and politics: a study of the relations between the Army and political process in Nigeria." In K. Kirkwood, ed. African Affairs (St. Antony's Papers), III (1969), 113-39.


_____ "Nigeria, Ghana and the world," Venture (Feb. 1969), 9-12.


_____ "Nigeria: the task of conflict resolution," World Today (July 1968), 269-80.


Doorn, Jacques van. Military profession and military regimes: commitments and conflicts: papers from a conference held in London on Sept. 14-16, 1967. The Hague: Mouton, 1968. 304 p.


Dudley, Billy J. "The Military in the new states of Africa," Nigerian J. Econ. Soc. Stud., VI (Nov. 1964), 351-61.


Ewelukwa, D. "The Constitutional aspects of the military take-over in Nigeria," Nigerian Law J., II, No. 1 (1967), 1-15.


Finer, S. E. The Man on the horse back: the role of the military in politics. New York: Praeger, 1962. 268 p.


Greene, Fred. "Toward understanding military coups," Africa Report, XI (Feb. 1966), 10-11; 14.
Observes that "a military take-over can be viewed as a step in the arduous search for order and progress, but at the same time it may be a setback in the process of maturation." Various motives for military coups in Africa are analyzed.

(THE MILITARY RULE - OBJECTIVES AND PROBLEMS)

Grundy, K. W. <u>Conflicting images of the military in Africa</u>. Nairobi: Makerere University College, 1968. 57 p. (Short studies and reprint series, 1.)


_____ "The Negative image of Africa's military," <u>Rev. Pol.</u> (Oct. 1968), 428-39.


Gutteridge, William. <u>Armed forces in new states</u>. London: Oxford University Press, 1962. 68 p.


_____ "Military elites in Ghana and Nigeria," <u>African Forum</u>, II (Summer 1966), 31-41.


_____ <u>The Military in African politics</u>. London: Methuen, 1969. 166 p. (Studies in African history, 4.)
Rev: <u>Afr. Stud.</u>, XXX, No. 1 (1971), 61-2.


_____ <u>Military institutions and power in the new states.</u> New York: Praeger, 1965. 182 p.
Rev: <u>Pacific Affairs</u>, XXXVIII (Fall/Winter 1965/66), 465.


_____ "Political role of African armed forces: the impact of foreign assistance," <u>African Affairs</u>, LXVI (April 1967), 93-103.


_____ "Die Ursprünge militärischer Staatsstreiche," <u>Europa Archiv</u>, II (Jan. 25, 1967), 63-72.


Hamon, L., ed. <u>Le Rôle extra-militaire de l'armée dans le tiers monde</u>. Paris: Presses Universitaires de France, 1967. 490 p.


Hayder, F. "Who's who in the Nigerian crisis," <u>Afrique Nouvelle</u> (Paris), No. 28 (May 1968), 40-3.


_____ "Civil-military relations in developing countries," <u>Brit. J. Soc.</u>, XVII (June 1966), 165-82.

(THE MILITARY RULE - OBJECTIVES AND PROBLEMS)

Huntington, S. P., ed. <u>Changing patterns of military politics</u>. New York: Free Press of Glencoe, 1962. 272 p.

Janowitz, Morris. <u>The Military in the political development of new nations: an essay in comparative analysis</u>. Chicago: University of Chicago Press, 1964. 134 p.
Civil-military relationships in the new states.
Rev: <u>Amer. Pol. Sci. Rev.</u>, LVIII (Dec. 1964), 977.
     <u>Pol. Sci. Q.</u>, LXXX, (Sept. 1965), 481.
Johnson, J. J., ed. <u>The Role of the military in underdeveloped countries</u>. Princeton: Princeton University Press, 1962. 427 p.
Rev: <u>Amer. Pol. Sci. Rev.</u>, LVI (Dec. 1962), 1019.
     <u>TLS</u> (Sept. 21, 1962), 732.
Keay, E. A. "Legal and constitutional changes in Nigeria under the Military Government," <u>J. Afr. Law</u>, X (Summer 1966), 92-105.

Lee, J. M. <u>African armies and civil order.</u> New York: Praeger, 1969. 198 p. (Institute for Strategic Studies. Studies in international security, 13.)
Rev: <u>Amer. Pol. Sci. Rev.</u>, LXIV (June 1970), 599.
     <u>Choice</u>, VI (Dec. 1969), 1484.

Lindsay, Kennedy. "Nigeria's Colonel Adekunle," In <u>Symposium on Nigeria - Biafra crisis</u>, African Studies Association, St. Augustine, University of West Indies, 1969. (Background paper, No. 2) 4 p.

"The Love-hate of five Nigerian colonels," <u>Economist</u>, CCXXII (March 18, 1967), 1021-2.
The attitudes of the Nigerian military leaders towards one another just before the Biafran secession.

Luckham, Alexander Robin. "Institutional transfer and breakdown in a new nation: the Nigerian military," <u>Adm. Sci. Q.</u>, XVI (Dec. 1971), 387-405.
This revised version of a conference paper examines the breakdown in the Nigerian military discipline during the two coups of 1966, illuminating the problems faced by the new countries in the creation of new military organizations. Bibliography and tables.

# Nigerian Civil War: An Annotated Bibliography

(THE MILITARY RULE - OBJECTIVES AND PROBLEMS)


Luckham, Alexander Robin.  The Nigerian military; a sociological analysis of authority and revolt, 1960-67.  Cambridge: Cambridge University Press, 1971.  376 p. (African Studies series.)
"This book is about a human tragedy of terrible proportions... To be sure, my analysis of events is bound to be influenced to some extent by my political biases. But I have tried to keep these to the minimum, or at the very least to make them explicit when they do occur." (Preface).  A revision of author's doctoral dissertation, University of Chicago, 1969, it examines the two military coups of January and July 1966; the military as a social system; and the role of the military in politics. Appendix 2 includes extracts from documents concerning the Aburi meeting of Nigerian military leaders in Ghana, Jan. 4-5, 1967.  The author is Lecturer in Sociology at Harvard University.


_____  "The Nigerian military: disintegration or integration?"  In S. K. Panter-Brick, ed.  Nigerian politics and military rule: prelude to the civil war.  London: Athlone, 1970,  pp. 58-77.


"Military coups in Africa,"  Afr. Inst. Bull., IV, No. 2 (1966), 23-9.


Miners, N. J.  The Nigerian Army, 1956-66.  London: Methuen, 1971.  290 p.


Muffett, D. J. M.  "The Nationalization of tribalism: some problems confronting the military regime in Nigeria,"  Seminar Paper, Pittsburgh, 1970.


Murray, D. J.  "The Western Nigerian civil service through political crisis and military coups,"  Seminar Paper, London University, 1969.


Murray, R.  "Militarism in Africa,"  New Left Review (London),  No. 38  (1966), 35-59.


"New Ironsides,"  Newsweek, LXVII (Jan. 31, 1966), 43-4.
The assumption of power by General Aguiyi-Ironsi, an Ibo, as Head of the Federal Military Government on Jan. 16, 1966.

(THE MILITARY RULE - OBJECTIVES AND PROBLEMS)


Newbury, Colin W. "Military intervention and political change in West Africa," Africa Quarterly, VII (Oct./Dec. 1967), 215-21.


Niesel, W. and M. Pradervand. "Call to prayer for peace in Nigeria, (document)," Ref. Presb. World, XXX (March 1968), 28-9.


Nigeria. Federal Ministry of Information. Guide to the National Military Government. Lagos, 1966. 30 p.


_____ Soldier of honour. Apapa: Nigerian National Press, 1968. 28 p.
General Yakubu Gowon, Head of Nigerian Military Government since August 1, 1966.


Nigeria, Western State. Report of the Commission of Inquiry into the Civil Disturbances which occurred in certain parts of the Western State of Nigeria in the month of December 1968, and other matters incidental thereto or connected therewith. Ibadan: Govt. Printer, 1969. 182 p.


Nigeria, Western State. Ministry of Home Affairs and Information. Fajuyi the Great: a soldier of peace. Ibadan, 1967. 23 p.


_____ Four decades of useful life. Ibadan, 1968. 22 p.
In commemoration of the 40th birth anniversary of Brigadier Adebayo, Military Governor of the Western State, on March 9, 1968.


_____ Lieutenant Colonel Adekunle Fajuyi: memorial brochure. Ibadan, 1967. 21 p.
Lieutenant Fajuyi was former Military Governor of Western Nigeria who was assassinated on July 29, 1966, along with General Ironsi, Head of the Military Government at the time.


_____ Towards return of civilian rule: civil commissioners join military government in Western State of Nigeria. Ibadan, 1967. 16 p.
Includes biographical information on the commissioners.

(THE MILITARY RULE - OBJECTIVES AND PROBLEMS)

Nigeria, Western State. Ministry of Home Affairs and Information. Western State, 1967; a review of the achievements of the Military Government of Western State of Nigeria. Ibadan, 1968. 60 p.

Nkrumah, Kwame. Handbook of revolutionary warfare: a guide to the armed phase of the African revolution. New York: International Publishers, 1968. 122 p.

Nord, E. Militärkupper; Afrika. Uppsala: Scandinavian Institute of African Studies, 1967. 23 p. (mimeographed).

Obilade, A. O. "Reform of customary court systems in Nigeria under the military government," J. Afr. Law, (Spring 1969), 28-44.

Ohonbamu, O. Nigeria: the Army and the people's cause. Ibadan: African Education Press, 1966. 54 p.

"One Nigerian," West Africa, No. 2747 (Jan. 24, 1970), 97.
Profile of General Gowon.

Otubushin, Ch. O. The Role of Federal Military Government today. Yaba: Pacific Printers, 1966. 32 p.

Sieve, Harold. "Can Nigeria afford its army?" Daily Telegraph, Oct. 26, 1971, p. 11.

Thompson, W. F. K. "General Gowon's real achievements," Daily Telegraph, Jan. 16, 1970, p. 18.
Lauds Gowon's tact, patience and moderation in re-unifying the country.

Tixier, G. "Los Gobiernos militares en Africa negra," Rev. Est. Pol., No. 156 (1967), 99-117.

Tukur, M. "Establishment of State Government in Northern Nigeria," J. Mod. Afr.

(THE MILITARY RULE - OBJECTIVES AND PROBLEMS)

Stud., VIII (April 1970), 128-33.


Welch, Claude Emerson. "Soldier and state in Africa," J. Mod. Afr. Stud., V, No. 3 (1967), 305-22.


_____ Soldier and state in Africa: a comparative analysis of military intervention and political change. Evanston, Ill.; Northwestern University Press, 1970. 320 p. The causes and implications of military intervention; the military and politics; the military and political change in Africa. Appendix A: Armed strength and defense expenditures of various African states in 1966. Appendix B: Violence and military involvement in politics from independence through 1968. Select bibliography.
Rev: Journal of Politics, XXXIV (May 1972), 679.
    World Politics, XXV (Jan. 1973), 309.

## THE WAR AND THE ECONOMY - OIL FACTOR

Aboyade, Ojetunji and A. Ayida. "The War economy in perspective," <u>Nigerian J. Econ. Soc. Stud.</u>, XIII (March 1971), 13-37.


Adebayo, R. **A.** <u>The Budget, programme and policy of the Western State Military Government for 1969-70. Broadcast delivered by Brigadier R. A. Adebayo, on 22nd May 1969.</u> Ibadan: Ministry of Home Affairs and Information, 1969. 18 p.


\_\_\_\_\_ <u>A Call for sacrifice: budget speech</u> (Programme and policy for the Western State Military Government), 1968-69...
Ibadan: Ministry of Home Affairs and Information, 1968. 16 p.


Atimomo, Emiko. "Political conflicts and economic instability: the Nigerian case," <u>Fume</u> (Benin, Nigeria) (1969), 21-6.


Ayida, A. A. "The Economic consequences of the Nigerian Civil War," <u>Management in Nigeria</u> (March 1970), 171-6.


"Biafra: reprieve for eighteen," (Oil men), <u>Time</u>, XCIII (June 13, 1969), 44, 49.
The capture of 18 oil-men - 14 Italians, 3 West Germans, 1 Lebanese - by Biafran forces in June 1969, raised an international outcry when they were sentenced to death but later commuted.


"Can Nigeria pay for the war?" <u>West Africa</u>, No. 2741 (Dec. 13, 1969), 1495.
Dr. Clement Isong, Governor of the Central Bank of Nigeria, warns inflation might affect the Nigerian capacity to wage war, despite the country's vast resources.


Cohen, Robin. "The Army and trade unions in Nigerian politics," <u>Civilisations</u>, XIX, No. 2 (1969), 226-30.


\_\_\_\_\_ "The relationship between trade unions and politics in Nigeria," Doctoral Dissertation, Birmingham University, 1969, 350 p.
A study of the political role of labor, with emphasis on the organizational problems; the level of clan consciousness in Nigerian workers; 'political' strikes of 1945 and 1964; the military regime, etc.

(THE WAR AND THE ECONOMY - OIL FACTOR)

Cohen, Robin. "Trade Union dilemmas in the current situation," Nigerian Opinion, IV, Nos. 2 & 3 (Feb. & March 1968).

Coomassie, M. A. "Nigerian Industrial Development Bank Ltd. Statement by the Chairman," West Africa, No. 2759 (April 25, 1970), 466-7.

"The Cost of the war," West Africa, No. 2642 (Jan. 20, 1968), 57-8.

"The Crisis and inter-regional trade," Nigerian Opinion, II, No. 11 (1966), 124-6.

"Crise économique," Afrique Express (Bruxelles), VIII (June 25, 1968), 7-8.

"The Economy and the war," West Africa, No. 2663 (June 15, 1968), 683; No. 2664 (June 22, 1968), 718.

"Financing Biafra's war," West Africa, No. 2658 (May 11, 1968), 543-4; No. 2681 (Oct. 19, 1968), 1228-9; No. 2683 (Nov. 2, 1968), 1290-1; No. 2686 (Nov. 23, 1968), 1375.

Fitch, Robert and Mary Oppenheimer. "Let them eat oil," Ramparts Magazine, VII (Sept. 7, 1968), 34-8.
Examination of the political significance of the oil concentrated in the secessionist territory by authors of Ghana: end of an illusion. (1966).

Godfrey, E. M. "West Africa: the economics of military rule," Banker (Lond.), CXVII (April 1967), 328-31.

Gowon, Yakubu. Building a great and happier nation: text of the national (1970-71) budget broadcast by Major General Yakubu Gowon. Lagos: Federal Ministry of Information, 1970. 10 p.

Hunter, Frederic. "Nigeria buoys economy amid war," Christian Sci. Mon.,

(THE WAR AND THE ECONOMY - OIL FACTOR)

Aug. 20, 1969, p. 4.

_____ "Self-confidence marks post-war Nigeria," Christian Sci. Mon., Oct. 20, 1971, pp. 9-14, 17.
Self-confidence is seen as Nigeria's greatest asset in its reconstruction task. Reviews the political and economic situation in the major states of Nigeria, especially the East Central State, and Nigeria's foreign policy.

Isong, Clement. "The Economy and the war," West Africa, No. 2663 (June 15, 1968), 683; No. 2664 (June 22, 1968), 718.
The author is Governor of the Central Bank of Nigeria.

Jervis, Steven. "Biafra has oil as well as starving children," New Republic, CLX (March 11, 1969), 8-10.
A former American Lecturer at the University of Nigeria, the author, opposed to the secession, reviews various relief operations, concluding that "despite wide public pressure and Mr. Nixon's sympathetic remarks, Washington is unlikely to be more deeply committed."

Johnson, M. O. Budget statement of Colonel Mobolaji O. Johnson, Military Governor of Lagos State for the Year 1969/70, on June 5, 1969. Lagos: Governor's Office, 1965. 35 p.

Latour, Henri. "L'Afrique et le pétrole," Afrique Nouvelle (Feb. 12-18, 1970), 8-9.

Lewis, A. W. Reflections on Nigeria's economic growth. Paris: Development Centre Studies, OECD, 1967. 65 p.

Lewis, J. R. "The Mineral industry of Nigeria," In Bureau of Mines and Minerals yearbook, 1967. Washington, D. C.; U. S. Dept. of Interior, 1968, pp. 1-9.

Lukacs, L. E. and E. Vielrose. "A Tentative projection of the structure of the Nigerian economy in 1976," Nigerian J. Econ. Soc. Stud., XII (March 1970), 3-28.

(THE WAR AND THE ECONOMY - OIL FACTOR)


Melson, Robert F. "Political dilemmas of Nigerian labor," Paper presented at the Annual Meeting of the African Studies Association, New York, November 1967, 26 p.


_____ "The Relationship between Government and Labor in Nigeria," Doctoral Dissertation, Massachusetts Institute of Technology, 1967.


Murcier, Alain. "Pétrole et guerre au Nigéria," Rev. Fr. Etud. Pol. Afr., (Nov. 1969), 51-60.


Nigeria. Federal Ministry of Information. Investment Opportunities in Nigeria. Lagos, 1967. 44 p.


"Nigeria: post-war economic reconstruction," Afr. Res. Bull., VI (March 31, 1969), 1276-7.


"Nigeria: 'sovereignty' muddle," West Africa, No. 2736 (Nov. 8, 1969), 1353-4. Biafra considers its security more important than sovereignty, and supports any peace talks without pre-conditions. See also page 1325.


"Nigeria: trente millions de tonnes de pétrole en jeu," Rev. Fr. Etud. Pol. Afr., No. 23 (Nov. 1967), 17-18.


"Nigerian oil in the balance," Petroleum Press Service (June 1967), 208-10. The political impact of oil and the difficulties of the petroleum companies during the war.


"Nigeria's reconstruction program will expand business opportunities," Commerce Today, I (Feb. 22, 1971), 46-8.


"Nigeria's trade unions in transition," West Africa, No. 2650 (March 16, 1968), 308-9; No. 2651 (March 23, 1968), 339. Stresses the need for a new labor legislation, outlining the functions of the five

(THE WAR AND THE ECONOMY - OIL FACTOR)

major labor unions. Some of their moves for mergers and their position in the war.

Ntamere, Charles Chijoke. "The Feasibility of an integrated iron and steel industry in Nigeria and Biafra," Doctoral Dissertation, University of Notre Dame, 1970. 268 p.
Utilizes the indigenous resources of iron and fuel to determine the viability of an integrated iron and steel industry.

"Oil and Biafra," Manchester Guardian, Aug. 21, 1969, pp. 12-13.

The Oil-rich Rivers State: account of mineral exploration and production in the Rivers State. Lagos: Office of the Governor, Information Unit, 1967. 29 p.

Phillips, Adedotun. "Nigeria's federal financial experience," J. Mod. Afr. Stud., IX (Oct. 1971), 389-408.

Rake, Alan and J. D. Farrell. "Nigeria's economy: no longer a model," Africa Report, XII (Oct. 1967), 19-22.
The effect of the war on oil production.

"Russia and steel plan," West Africa, No. 2687 (Nov. 30, 1968), 1415.

"Russians criticize Nigerian economy," African Review (May 1969), 5-7.

Schatz, Sayre P. "A Look at the balance sheet; petroleum smooths the way for the economic recovery from the effects of the war but what about the future?" Africa Report, XV (Jan. 1970), 18-21.
With the aid of charts and tables, the author, Professor of Economics at Temple University in the U.S.A., examines the place of the peasant-produced agricultural products and petroleum industry in the Nigerian economy.

Schatzl, L. "The Development of the oil industry in Nigeria; with special reference to the effects of the Civil War," Erdkunde (March 1970), 59-71.

(THE WAR AND THE ECONOMY - OIL FACTOR)

_____ Petroleum in the Nigerian economy. Ibadan: Oxford University Press for the Nigerian Institute of Social and Economic Research, 1969. 278 p.


_____ Selected aspects of the Nigerian energy economy. Ibadan: Nigerian Institute of Social and Economic Research, 1969. 20 p. (mimeographed).


Sidenko, V. "Oil war in Nigeria," New Times (Moscow) (March 15, 1967), 21-2.


Tanzer, M. The Political economy of international oil and the underdeveloped countries. London: Temple Smith, 1970. 435 p.


Thayer, G. The War business; the international trade in armaments. London: Weidenfeld & Nicolson, 1969. 417 p.
French edition under title: Les Marchands de Guerre. Paris: Julliard, 1969. 533 p.
German edition under title: Geschäfte mit Waffen und Krieg. Hamburg: Hoffman & Campe, 1970. 387 p.


"32 years of Nigerian oil," West Africa, No. 2750 (Feb. 21, 1970), 182-3.
Historical development of oil industry in Nigeria, outlining the interests of foreign companies.
"Tin and civil war," West Africa, No. 2668 (July 20, 1968), 840.


Traore, Diawa-Mory. "Industry growth and foreign trade in four West African countries: Ghana, Nigeria, the Ivory Coast and Senegal," Doctoral Dissertation, University of Pittsburgh, 1969. 205 p.


Ugo, Sylvester U. "Presidential address," Nigerian J. Econ. Soc. Stud., XIII (March 1971), 3-12.
A review of the economic possibilities and problems in Nigeria by the President of the Nigerian Economic Society.

(THE WAR AND THE ECONOMY - OIL FACTOR)

"War and economics in Nigeria," <u>Legon Observer</u>, III, No. 1 (1968), 11-12.
Maintains that the war was "distorting the Nigerian economy, for few, if any,
developing countries' economy can withstand the strain of a war of such proportions."
The situation was aggravated by British devaluation which resulted in Nigerian
devaluation.

# Nigerian Civil War: An Annotated Bibliography

## THE WAR AND FOREIGN COUNTRIES - GENERAL

### General

Aluko, Olajide. "Ghana and the Nigerian civil war," Nigerian J. Econ. Soc. Stud., XII (Nov. 1970), 341-60.

Auspitz, Josiah. "Biafra and the bureaucrats," Ripon Forum (Feb. 1969), 5-11. Contends that the foreign powers with political and economic axes to grind were opposed to the secession.

"The Biafra blunder: Trudeau's No. 1 embarrassment in No. 2 man, Unflappable Mr. Sharp," National Observer, (U.S.), Oct. 28, 1968, p. 6. Sharp is Canada's Foreign Minister.

Brewin, Andres and David MacDonald. Canada and the Biafran tragedy. Toronto: James Lewis and Samuel, 1970. 173 p. Completed in December 1969, just before the Biafran surrender, it was designed to help "influence the Canadian government and others to press for a cease fire and a negotiated peace through the United Nations and to initiate more extensive relief operations." (Preface)

"Canada, the impact of the Biafra phenomenon," Time, XCII (Nov. 15, 1968), 19.

"China's support for Biafra," African Review (Nov. 1968), 5-7.

"Conscience is his co-pilot: the story of Count Carl Gustaf von Rosen, a Swedish nobleman who became a flying angel of mercy wherever people were suffering," Reader's Digest, XCV (Dec. 1969), 207-8. Count Carl von Rosen helped to bring relief to the Abyssinians when Mussolini of Italy attacked them in 1935-36 and to the Fins when attacked by the Russians in 1942.

Cooley, J. K. East wind over Africa: Red China's offensive. New York: Walker, 1965. 245 p.

# Nigerian Civil War: An Annotated Bibliography

(THE WAR AND FOREIGN COUNTRIES - GENERAL)

Cronje, Suzanne. The World and Nigeria. London: Sidwick and Jackson, 1972. 352 p.
A critical study of the Nigerian and Biafran leadership and foreign involvement in
the war. The author is co-author of Biafra: Britain's shame (1969).
Rev: West Africa, No. 2893 (Nov. 20, 1972), 1559 & 1561.


"Declaration du Gouvernement gabonais sur Biafra," Afrique Express (Bruxelles),
VIII (May 25, 1968), 10.


Decraene, P. "Repercussions of Nigerian crisis in Dahomey," Africa Quarterly,
VII, No. 3 (1967), 212-24.


Dike, Chijioke. "Le Biafra et les grandes puissances," Rev. Fr. Etud. Pol. Afr.
(Jan. 1970), 69-78.


Euben, J. Peter. "Nationalist and Communist Chinese foreign policy in Asia, Africa
and Latin America," Master's Thesis, University of California, Berkeley, 1964.
229 p.


Foell, Earl. "The World's deadly silence on Nigeria," Los Angeles Times, March
16, 1969, Section G, p. 3.
The U.N. impasse regarding the war and the extent of foreign involvement.


Garrison, Lloyd. "Big Powers hold the key in a proxy war," N.Y. Times, March 23,
1969, p. 2.


Gingyera-Pinyewa, A. G. C. "Sozialismus und Kalter Krieg in Schwarzafrika,"
Moderne Welt, X, No. 2 (1969), 172-81.


Hevi, E. J. The Dragon's embrace: the Chinese Communists and Africa. London:
Pall Mall Press, 1966, 152 p.


Houphouet-Boigny, Felix. "Biafra: a human problem, a human tragedy," African
Scholar (Washington, D.C.), (Nov. 1968), 10-13.

(THE WAR AND FOREIGN COUNTRIES - GENERAL)

The author is President of the Ivory Coast, one of the four African states to recognize Biafra.

Huff, Curtis E. "Political development and foreign policy: problems in the African countries," Doctoral Dissertation, Michigan State University, 1968?

Idang, Gordon J. "Nigerian political process and foreign policy," Doctoral Dissertation, State University of New York, 1970.

_____ "The Politics of Nigerian foreign policy; the ratification and renunciation of the Anglo-Nigerian Defence Agreement," Afr. Stud. Rev., XIII (Sept. 1970), 227-51.
The Anglo-Nigerian Defence pact was approved by the Federal House of Representatives on November 14, 1960.

Ituen, Edet Bassey. "Nigerian foreign relations: a study of the factors influencing Nigerian foreign relations after independence," Doctoral Dissertation, St. Louis University (U.S.), 1970. 421 p.
Nigeria's political disposition towards the West rather than the East is mainly due to its historical ties with the former, particularly Great Britain. Nigeria is likely to maintain a clear-cut non-alignment policy following the civil war.

"Ivory Coast ousts former Biafran Chief," N.Y. Times, Oct. 9, 1970, p. 3.
A rumor that the former Biafran leader, Odumegwu Ojukwu, might be expelled from the Ivory Coast for making political statements on the war. He has been given a political asylum there on condition that he eschews all political activities or statements.

McKay, Vernon, ed. African diplomacy: studies in the determination of foreign policy. New York: Praeger, 1966. 210 p.
Rev: Amer. Pol. Sci. Rev., LXI (Sept. 1967), 839.

"The Meaning of Count von Rosen," Christian Sci. Mon., June 7, 1969, p. E.
The celebrated but enigmatic Swedish aviator who featured prominently in the war.

# Nigerian Civil War: An Annotated Bibliography

(THE WAR AND FOREIGN COUNTRIES - GENERAL)

Mhando, S. "Imperialism on credit and the war in Nigeria by proxy," Pan-African Journal, III (Winter 1970), 14-24.
The author is Minister of State for Foreign Affairs of Tanzania.

Morel, Y. "La Guerre du Nigéria vue par les pays enrichis," Tam-Tam (Paris) (Feb. 1969), 15-23.

"Murder by proxy in Biafra," Spotlight on Africa (Aug. 1968), 1-2.

Nielsen, W. A. The Great Powers and Africa. London: Pall Mall Press, 1969. 431 p.
Rev: Choice, VII (March 1970), 152.
New York Times Book Review (Jan. 25, 1970), 3.
Nigeria. Federal Ministry of Information. Foreign meddlers in the Nigerian crisis. Lagos, 1968. 8 p.

_____ That is false, Nyerere. Lagos, 1969. 15 p.
The Nigerian Federal Government denounces the action of President Julius Nyerere of Tanzania in according Biafra a full diplomatic recognition in April 1968, since such a recognition contradicts the principles of the Organisation of African Unity.

"Nigeria-Tanzania's intervention," Afr. Res. Bull., V, No. 4 (1968), 1040-5.

Nyerere, Julius. "Why Tanzania recognized Biafra," Africa Report, XIII (June 1968), 27.
Reviews the circumstances of the Biafran secession, the concept of African unity, and argues that the Biafrans have been rejected by other Nigerians and contends that "unity can only be based on the general consent of the people governed - Once a large number of the people of any political government stop believing that the state is theirs, and that the government is their instrument, then the unit is no longer viable."

"Nyerere and Nigeria's war," West Africa, No. 2655 (April 20, 1968), 451.
The impact of the Tanzanian recognition of Biafra on the war.

"Nyerere franchit le Rubicon," Jeune Afrique, No. 381 (April 28, 1968), 12-13.
President Julius Nyerere was the first African leader to recognize Biafra in April 1968.

(THE WAR AND FOREIGN COUNTRIES - GENERAL)

Obiahegbon, P. "The countries behind Ojukwu's rebellion," Towards One Nigeria (Lagos), No. 3 (1967), 71-2.


Ogum, Onyemaeke. "The Ghanaian press and the Nigerian crisis," Legon Observer, III, No. 7 (1968), 6-8.


Ortiz, Eduardo. "Las Grandes potencias y la crisis de Nigeria," Est. Int., III (April/June 1969), 63.


Post, James. "Canadians renew demands for Biafra policy shift," Christian Sci. Mon., Dec. 8, 1969, p. 9.
Mounting pressure on the Canadian Government to intercede in the conflict.


Rivkin, A. African presence in world affairs. London: Collier-Macmillan, 1963. 304 p.
Rev: Current History, XLVIII (April 1965), 235.


"Russes et Britanniques se surveillent," Jeune Afrique (Paris), No. 412 (Dec. 1, (1968), 23.


Sanness, J. "Nigeria-Biafra and Norway," Internasjonal Politikk (Oslo), No. 3 (1969), 306-9.


Scalapino, Robert A. "Sino-Soviet competition in Africa," Foreign Affairs, XLI (July 1964), 640-54.


Schwarz, Walter. "Foreign powers and the Nigerian war," Africa Report, XV (Feb. 1970), 12-14.
One of the best written articles on the roles of the major powers in the war by a British journalist, author of Nigeria (1968) which includes one of the most objective studies of the background to the war.


Tanzania. Tanzania Government's statement on the recognition of Biafra. Dar-es-Salaam: Govt. Printer, 1968. 6 p.

(THE WAR AND FOREIGN COUNTRIES - FRANCE)

Tanzania, an East African country, was the first African state to recognize Biafra on April 13, 1968.

Widstrand, C. G.  The Soviet bloc, China and Africa.  Uppsala: Scandinavian Institute of African Affairs, 1964.  202 p.

### France

Barnes, J.  "Enter Charles de Gaulle; French sponsored arms shipments to Biafra," Newsweek, LXXII (Nov. 18, 1968),  74 +.
The French President who publicly declared his support for Biafra denied any arms to the secessionist state.

"Biafra - les raisons de la France," Jeune Afrique (Paris),  No. 373  (Feb. 26, 1968), 20.

Breene, A.  "Francophone Africa," African Affairs,  LXVI (Jan. 1967),  12-19.

Crocker, Ch.  "France's changing military interests," Africa Report, XIII (June 1968),  16-41.

Decreane, Philippe.  "La Politique africaine du général de Gaulle," Rev.  Fr.  Etud. Pol.  Afr.  (Nov. 1969),  73-89.

Dedenuola, J.  "The French and the rebels," Nigerian Opinion,  V,  Nos. 8-10 (1969), 463-5.

France.  Ministère des Affaires Etrangères.  La France et le Biafra.  Paris, 1969. 28 p.

(THE WAR AND FOREIGN COUNTRIES - FRANCE)

"France and Africa now," West Africa, No. 2667 (July 13, 1968), 797-8.

"France and Nigerian crisis," West Africa, No. 2648 (March 2, 1968), 243-4.
An informative article analyzing the positions of the French press in the war and the probable reasons for the French support of Biafra.

"France supports Biafra's case," West Africa, No. 2670 (Aug. 3, 1968), 909.
French support is considered both political and economic.

"France's stake in Nigeria," West Africa, No. 2671 (Aug. 1968), 929, 938.

"French offer only limited support to rebels, Biafra leader claims," Washington Post, Aug. 23, 1969, p. A 11.
A report that the Biafran leader admitted French assistance, even if limited.

Herr, Maurice. "La France et le Biafra," Afrique Nouvelle (Jan. 29-Feb. 4, 1970), 6.
Reviews the role of France in the war and its support of Biafra.

Mortimer, E. France and the Africans, 1944-1960: a political history. London: Faber & Faber, 1969. 390 p.

Obanya, P. "France and the Nigeria crisis," Afrique Actuelle, No. 32 (Oct. 1968), 33-4.

"Pourquoi des Français portent tant d'intérêt aux petits ex-Biafrais qui sont au Gabon?" Afrique Nouvelle (Aug. 20-26, 1970), 6.
Gabon was one of the four African countries to recognize Biafra. A former French colony, Gabon which still maintains close political ties with France, did most to harbour many Biafran children evacuated from the war zone.

Whiteman, K. "France's year in Africa," In Colin Legum and J. Drysdale, eds. Africa contemporary record: annual survey and documents. London: Africa Research, 1969, pp. 27-31.

# Nigerian Civil War: An Annotated Bibliography

(THE WAR AND FOREIGN COUNTRIES - GREAT BRITAIN)

### Great Britain

Akinyemi, A. B. "The British press and the Nigerian Civil War," African Affairs, LXXI (Oct. 1972), 408-26.
Critical of the British press for its editorial support of Biafra, it concludes "this was not an honourable era in Britich journalism. The news was often incorrect and misleading, while editorial opinions ... demonstrated a naiveté in elementary international politics."

Barnes, Michael. "Biafra: why we must think again." Observer (London), March 9, 1969, p. 10.
Argues that the protracted nature of the war should make the British Government re-examine its total support of the Nigerian Federal Government.

"Blame for Biafra," Observer (London), Nov. 30, 1969, p. 10.
Letters to the editor, majority of which criticize the role of the British Government in the war.

"Britain's role in Nigeria," Manchester Guardian, Nov. 22, 1969, p. 12.
An editorial urging the British Government to re-evaluate its lack of neutrality in the conflict in the light of the grim determination of the Biafrans to hold on indefinitely despite starvation.

Brockway, F. "My views on Biafra and Nigeria," Tribune (London), Jan. 3, 1969, p. 7.

Brown, Neville. "Nigeria; the arms supply," Venture (July 1969), 8-10.

_____ "Why Britain didn't stop the Nigerian war," New Society, (July 19, 1968), 85-6.

Churchill, Winston. "Britain's role in Biafra tragedy," San Francisco Chronicle, March 17, 1969, p. 1+.
The grandson of late Winston Churchill, former Prime Minister of Britain, contends that the protraction of the war and the magnitude of the human tragedy were due to the British support of the Federal Government.

(THE WAR AND FOREIGN COUNTRIES - GREAT BRITAIN)

"The Commons and Nigeria," West Africa, No. 2703 (March 22, 1969), 330.
The debate in the British House of Commons on the war.

"Commonwealth and Nigeria," West Africa, No. 1692 (Jan. 4, 1969), 1-2.
The attitudes of countries of the British Commonwealth to the crisis.

"The Crisis and the British," West Africa, No. 2668 (July 20, 1968), 878.
The position of the British Government in the war.

Cronje, Suzanne. "Our man in Nigeria," New Statesman, LXXXII (Oct. 22, 1971),
529-30.
Major Walsworth-Bell, British member of the international observer team.

Dudley, Billy J. "The Commonwealth and the Nigeria/Biafra conflict," In Seminar
papers on the impact of African issues on the Commonwealth. London: Institute of
Commonwealth Studies, 1969, pp. 14-30.

"Ending war in Nigeria; Britain's duty," Times (London), Nov. 13, 1969, p. 9.
Contends that the suspension of the British arms shipments to Nigeria would hasten
the end of the war.

Forsyth, Frederick. "Remedies for Biafra," Illus. Lond. News, CCLV (July 12,
1969), 17-19.
"The Policy of the British Government is one of whole-hearted support for the
Federal Nigerian government in its efforts to solve the present crisis of unity by
force rather than negotiation." Examines over-all British policy in the war.

Great Britain. Colonial Office. Conflict in Nigeria; the British view; some questions
answered and an account of the shaping of modern Nigeria. London: H.M.S.O.,
1969, 26 p.

_____ Nigeria: No. 1; report of the observer team to Nigeria, Sept. 24-Nov. 23, 1968.
London: H.M.S.O., 1970. 36 p. (Cmnd. 3878)

Hanbury, H. G. Biafra: a challenge to the conscience of Britain. London: Britain-
Biafra Association, 1968. 19 p.

(THE WAR AND FOREIGN COUNTRIES - GREAT BRITAIN)

Hanning, Hugh. "Britain's part in the Nigerian war," Round Table, LIX (July 1969), 249-54.

"Harold Wilson's arms," West Africa, No. 2702 (March 15, 1969), 289-90.
The political significance of the British arms in the civil war.

Hatch, John. "Nigeria, Biafra and Britain," New Statesman (Jan. 9, 1970), 40-3.

Hayder, F. "English people faced with the war of Biafra," Afrique Actuelle, No. 31 (Sept. 1968), 41-3.

Ibiam, Akanu. "Britain - and the black," Atlas, XVIII (July 1969), 52-3.
Accuses Britain of using a double standard in dealing with white and black people in Africa, as shown by the British squeamishness in quelling the Rhodesian rebellion by force, and its support of the Federal Nigeria's use of force to crush the Biafran secession. The author, an Ibo, is former Governor of Eastern Nigeria.

Legum, Colin. "Anglo-American talk on Biafra war," Observer (London), March 9, 1969, p. 9.

_____ "British policy towards Africa," Venture, XX (Oct. 1968), 6-11.

_____ "Britain's year in Africa," In Colin Legum and J. Drysdale, eds. Africa contemporary record: annual survey and documents. London: Africa Research, 1969, pp. 22-6.

Lewis, Roy. "Britain and Biafra," Round Table, LX (July 1970), 241-8.

_____ "Colonel Ojukwu's secession raises dilemma for the Government over recognition issue. Britain's danger of antagonizing both sides in Nigeria," Times (London), May 31, 1967, p. 10.
The political dilemma of the British Government over the question of recognizing the former Eastern Region on its secession from the Federation as Biafra on May 30, 1967.

(THE WAR AND FOREIGN COUNTRIES - GREAT BRITAIN)

"M. P.'s and Biafra," West Africa, No. 2664 (June 22, 1968), 713; No. 2665
(June 29, 1968), 739.
Debate in the British Parliament over Britain's arms shipments to Nigeria.


Maclean, D. British foreign policy since Suez, 1956-1968. London: Hodder & Stough-
ton, 1970. 343 p.
Africa south of the Sahara, pp. 197-228.
Rev: Economist, CCXXXV (May 9, 1970), 47.
TLS (April 23, 1970), 449.
Murray, David J. "Britain's influence in Africa," Current History, LIII (May 1967),
276-81.
Evaluation of Britain's relationship with its former African colonies.


Ofonagoro, Walter. "The Anglo-Nigerian harassment of Biafra," Pan African J.,
(Spring 1968), 120-4.


Ojedokun, O. "Nigeria's relations with the Commonwealth with special reference to
her relations with the United Kingdom, 1960-1966," Doctoral Dissertation, London
University, 1968.


"Pourquoi Londres soutient tant Lagos?" Afrique Nouvelle, (Dec. 4-10, 1969), 6.
Attempts to explain why the British Government was in support of use of force by the
Nigerian Government to crush the Biafran secession.


"Six and Biafra," Times (London), August 6, 1969, p. 6.
Argues that the British support of the Nigerian Government could damage Britain's
chances of entering the European Common Market - a view first expressed in an
article in Le Monde, by Jean François Bonnier, Secretary-General of an Association
called Europe-France-Afrique.


Smith, John Hilary. Colonial cadet in Nigeria. Durham: Duke University Press, 1968.
202 p. (Commonwealth Studies Center, publication No. 24.)


"Tragic decline of Britain's share," West Africa, No. 2742 (Dec. 20, 1969), 1551.

(THE WAR AND FOREIGN COUNTRIES -  THE SOVIET UNION)

Waugh, Auberon and Suzanne Cronje.  Biafra: Britain's shame.  London: Michael
  Joseph, 1969,  118 p.
  Provides background account of the war; and examines various peace efforts, the
  position of African states and the Organization of African Unity, involvement of
  foreign powers.  Critical of the Nigerian war policy and British support of it.
  Rev: West Africa,  No. 2735 (Nov. 1, 1969),  1305-6.

"Wilson and Nigeria,"  West Africa,  No. 2705 (April 5, 1969),  373-4.
  The position of the British Prime Minister on the war.

"Wilson moves to start talks on Biafra,"  Times  (London),  Jan. 16, 1969,  p. 1.
  Harold Wilson's subsequent visit to Nigeria in March 1969, did not contribute to
  peace.

"Wilson seen as enemy,"  Times  (London),  March 20, 1969,  p. 7.
  Declared unqualified by Biafra to mediate in the conflict, the British Prime Minister
  was regarded as an enemy by the secessionists because of Britain's  support of
  Federal Nigeria.

### The Soviet Union

Bonavia, David.  "Soviet attitude on Nigerian war,"  Times  (London),  July 4, 1969,
  p. 8.
  The Soviet was strongly behind the Federal efforts to crush the secession, which,
  it claimed, was engineered by "imperialists. "

Cohn, Helen Desfosses.  Soviet policy toward black Africa: the focus on national
  integration.  New York: Praeger, 1972.  312 p.  (Praeger special studies in international politics and public affairs. )
  Rev: West Africa,  No. 2899 (Jan. 1, 1973),  11-13.
    Choice,  X (March 1970),  178.

Joshua, W. and S. P. Gilbert.  Arms for the Third World; Soviet military and diplomacy.  Baltimore:  Johns Hopkins Press, 1969. 169 p.

(THE WAR AND FOREIGN COUNTRIES - THE SOVIET UNION)

Klinghoffer, Arthur Jay. "Why the Soviets chose sides," Africa Report, XIII (Feb. 1968), 47-9.
Reasons for the Soviet support of Nigerian Federal Government.


Korovikov, V. "Nigerian crisis," Pravda, June 16, 1967, p. 5.
Attributes the military coup of January 15, 1966, to a Western plot.


Legvold, Robert M. "A Comparative study of Soviet policy toward six West African countries in the post-colonial period," Doctoral Dissertation, Fletcher School of Law and Diplomacy, Tufts University, 1967.
The countries studied are Ghana, the Ivory Coast, Mali, Nigeria, Senegal and Guinea.


_____ "Moscow's changing view of Africa's revolutionary regimes," Africa Report, XIV (March/April 1969), 54-8.


_____ Soviet policy in West Africa. Cambridge, Mass.: Harvard University Press, 1970. 372 p.
A revision of his doctoral dissertation.
Rev: Choice, VII (Dec. 1970), 1438.
     Library J., XCV (Nov. 1, 1970), 3788.


Morison, D. "Soviet Union and Africa, 1968," In Colin Legum and J. Drysdale, eds. Africa contemporary record. London: Africa Research, 1969, pp. 38-42.


Mosely, Philip E. "Soviet policy in the developing countries," Foreign Affairs, XLIII (Oct. 1964), 87-98.


Murarka, Dev. "Soviet aid for Nigeria pays off," Observer (London), Jan. 25, 1970, p. 2.
The Soviet-Nigerian friendship.


"Nigeria and Russian aid," African Review (Dec. 1968), 9-12.

(THE WAR AND FOREIGN COUNTRIES - THE SOVIET UNION)

"Nigeria: l'influence de Moscou augmente," Jeune Afrique (Paris), No. 366 (Jan. 14, 1968), 15.

"The Press testifies: false vs. genuine friends," Curr. Dig. Soviet Pr., XXI (July 23, 1969), 26.
The complete text from Izvestia, June 29, 1969, O. 2, claiming that the Nigerian Govt. newspaper Morning Post had uncovered the efforts of the Western "Imperialists" to destroy Soviet-Nigerian relations.

Ra'anan, U. The U.S.S.R. arms the Third World: case studies in Soviet foreign policy. Cambridge, Mass.: M. I. T. Press, 1969. 256 p.
Rev: Choice, VII (April 1970), 301.
   Library J., XCV (Feb. 15, 1970), 673.
Rubinstein, G. "Aspects of Soviet-African economic relations," J. Mod. Afr. Stud., VIII (Oct. 1970), 387-404.

"Russia in Africa," West Africa, No. 2699 (Feb. 22, 1969), 201-2.
The fear that Russia would gain a political foothold in West Africa because of its support of Nigeria.
"The Russians in Nigeria," West Africa, No. 2699 (Feb. 22, 1969), 203.
Despite the Soviet arms sales to Nigeria, the political, social and economic conditions in Nigeria are unsuitable to communist acceptance.
Schapiro, Leonard. "The Soviet dream in Africa," Encounter, XXIV (Feb. 1965), 49-53.

Solodovnikov, V. G. "The Soviet Union and Africa," New Times (Moscow), No. 21 (1969), 8-9.

"Soviet thoughts on Nigeria's crisis," Mizan, IX, No. 4 (1967), 174.

Tryagunenko, V. L. "Soviet view of Africa - difficulties and prospects," In Colin Legum and J. Drysdale, eds. Africa contemporary record. London: Africa Research, 1969, pp. 626-30.

Tryasunov, A. "Nigeria: war or peace," Int. Affairs (Moscow), No. 7 (1968), 89-90.

(THE WAR AND FOREIGN COUNTRIES - THE UNITED STATES)

"The U.S.S.R. and the war in Africa," <u>Mizan</u> (London), XI, No. 1 (1969), 31-8.

Zorza, Victor. "Kremlin sees Western 'plot' to split tribes," <u>Guardian</u> (Manchester), Jan. 28, 1970, p. 3.
The Soviet Union claims that Biafran secession was engineered by Western Powers.

## The United States

Baker, W. G. "The United States and Africa in the United Nations: a case study in American foreign policy," Doctoral Dissertation, University of Geneva, 1968. 241 p. (Thèse No. 189).

Beal, Christopher. "How the State Dept. watched Biafra starve," <u>Ripon Forum</u>, VI (March 1970), 8-12; 17-19.
Contends that the U.S. Govt.'s neutrality was pro-Federal Nigeria and that the U.S. should have overridden political niceties to bring in massive relief to Biafra. See reply by U.S. Under-Secretary of State on p. 28.

"Biafra getting worse: an editorial," <u>Life</u>, LXV (Dec. 20, 1968), 26B.
Questions the U.S. original assumption behind its Nigerian war policy and criticizes its neutrality.

Brookes, E. W. "African objectives and the United States policy," <u>Pan-African J.</u>, I, Nos. 2-3 (1968), 127-39.

Buckley, William. "U.S. Biafra performance was proper - but then..." <u>L.A. Times</u>, Jan. 19, 1970, part 2, p. 7.
Argues that while the U.S. neutrality was politically expedient, it might be morally questionable. The author is a well-known conservative American journalist.

Chapman, William. "Biafra lobby melds Left and Right," <u>Washington Post</u>, Jan. 19, 1969, pp. Al & Al4.

# Nigerian Civil War: An Annotated Bibliography

(THE WAR AND FOREIGN COUNTRIES - THE UNITED STATES)

The mounting public sympathy for Biafra in the United States is seen to have cut across ideological boundaries.

"Conscience or cynicism," Newsweek, LXXII (Dec. 16, 1968), 53-4.

"La Chute du Biafra a causé d'émoi aux Etats-Unies," Afrique Nouvelle (Jan. 29-Feb. 4, 1970), 6.

Cyr, Leo G. United States policy toward Africa. Athens: Center for International Studies, Ohio University, 1966, 23 p. (Papers in international studies, No. 1.)

Emerson, Rupert. Africa and United States policy. Englewood Cliffs, N. J.: Prentice-Hall, 1967. 117 p. Bibliog. (America's role in world affairs series.)
A survey of the U. S. relations with Africa south of the Sahara with emphasis on the last decade. The author is Professor of Government, Harvard University.
Rev: Choice, V (May 1968), 406.
       Amer. Hist. Rev., LXXIII (Dec. 1967), 446.

_____ "The Character of American interests in Africa," In W. Goldschmidt, ed. The United States and Africa. New York: Praeger, 1963, pp. 3-35.

Evans, Rowland and Robert Novak. "Biafra-Nigeria meddling," L.A. Times, Dec. 11, 1969. Part 2, p. 7.
Alleges that the U. S. Government was financing Nigeria in the construction of a road near the combat zone which could be militarily useful to the Federal forces.

Foell, Earl W. "Africa's vanishing act at the U.N.: where does the United States stand on African questions? Africa Report, XIV (Nov. 1969), 31-3.
The author is U.N. correspondent for the Los Angeles Times.

Goodell, Charles. "Biafra and the American conscience," Sat. Rev., LII (April 12, 1969), 24-7.
Urges U.S. to send massive relief to Biafra and help end the war.

# Nigerian Civil War: An Annotated Bibliography

(THE WAR AND FOREIGN COUNTRIES - THE UNITED STATES)


Goodell, Charles. "Report on Biafra: interview," New Yorker, XLV (April 12, 1969), 37-8.
Goodell's highly publicized but detailed report of his mission to Nigeria was made before the U.S. Senate on February 25, 1969.


Hovey, H. A. United States military assistance. New York: Praeger, 1965. 306 p.


Hunter, Frederic. "Nigeria and Biafra woo U.S." Christian Sci. Mon., Feb. 24, 1969, p. 6.


_____ "Nigeria, Biafra vie for U.S. hand," Christian Sci. Mon., April 12, 1969, p. 2.
The Federal and Biafran officials in U.S. try to win the support of the U.S. Government and the public.


Kennedy, Edward and Donald Lukens. "Time for Action on Biafra," Reader's Digest, XCIV (May 1969), 75-9.
A two-part article, by U.S. Senators who were both Biafran sympathizers, advocating U.S. relief supplies to Biafra even without Nigerian authorization.


Kramer, Morris. "Biafra; while America sleeps," Liberator (March 1969), 6-11.
Critical of Nigerian war policy and U.S. neutrality.


Legum, Colin. "The U.S. and Africa, 1968," In Colin Legum and J. Drysdale, eds. Africa contemporary record: annual survey and documents. London: Africa Research, 1969, pp. 32 -7.


McKay, V. "Changing external pressures on Africa," In W. Goldschmidt, ed. The United States and Africa. New York: Praeger, 1963, pp. 74-112.


Meisler, Stanley. "U.S. efforts in Nigerian war weighed." L.A. Times, Feb. 19, 1971, Part 1-A, pp. 1-3.
Critical evaluation of all U.S. relief efforts during the war.

(THE WAR AND FOREIGN COUNTRIES - THE UNITED STATES)

"Motives vary, but sentiment builds for Biafra," National Observer, (U.S.), Feb. 3, 1969, p. 3.
A dramatic description of the mounting American public and Congressional support for massive relief shipments to Biafra.

"Nixon's chance to end the Nigerian-Biafra war," Africa Today, XV, No. 6 (1969), 1-3.

"Nixon's new Africa," West Africa, No. 2751 (Feb. 28, 1970), 217-8.
Contends that despite the Soviet support of Nigeria, President Nixon is convinced that Africa is not a place for communism.

Ostrander, F. Taylor. "U.S. private investment in Africa," Africa Report, XIV (Jan. 1969), 38-41.
Includes statistical tables on total U.S. direct investment in Africa, investment by type of activity.

Palmer, Joseph. "Magnitude and complexity of the Nigerian problem," U.S. Dept. State Bull., LIX (Oct. 7, 1968), 357-62.
The U.S. Assistant Secretary of State for African Affairs contends that Africans must find a solution to African problems. Opposed to the secession, he reiterates the efforts of the Organization of African Unity to end the war.

_____ "Nigeria: United States position; address, Sept. 11, 1966," Vital Speeches, XXXV (Oct. 15, 1968), 15-18.
The former U.S. Ambassador to Nigeria restates U.S. neutrality in the conflict, and favors the preservation of the Nigerian territorial integrity.

"Policy on Nigeria/Biafra; Congress, public press for more Biafran relief," Congressional Quarterly Weekly Report, XXVII (April 4, 1969), 481-4.
One of the most informative articles analyzing official U.S. policy on the war, attitudes of the Congress and those of individual senators and congressmen, and the motivations of the major relief organizations that sprang up throughout the U.S.

"A Reply from Elliot L. Richardson," Ripon Forum, VI (March 1970), 28.
The U.S. Under-Secretary of State denies Christopher Beal's charge that the U.S. State Department deliberately watched Biafra starve and restates the U.S. policy on

(THE WAR AND FOREIGN COUNTRIES - THE UNITED STATES)


the war.
See pp. 8-12, 17-19 for Beal's charge.


U.S. Congress. House. Committee on Foreign Affairs. Subcommittee on Africa. The Post-war Nigerian situation: hearing, Jan. 27, 1970. (91st Congress, 2nd session), Washington, D.C., 1970. 21 p.


U.S. Dept. of Defense. Military assistance and foreign military sales facts. Washington, D.C., 1967.


"The U.S. and Nigeria," West Africa, No. 2715 (June 14, 1969), 678-9.


"U.S. regrets Soviet decision to supply arms to Nigeria," U.S. Dept. State Bull., (Sept. 11, 1967), 320.


Usenekong, N. "The Two faces of the United States," Towards One Nigeria (Lagos), No. 3 (1967), 66-8.

STARVATION AND RELIEF

Adam, Corinna. "Politics of charity," New Statesman, LXXVIII (July 4, 1969), 3-4. Advocates more British relief for the war affected areas and questions the legitimacy of starvation as a weapon of warfare.


"Africa and relief for Biafra," Legon Observer, IV, No. 16 (1969), 12-13.


Africa Concern. Joint Biafra famine appeal; first annual report. Dublin, 1969.


Africa Research Group. "The Politics of humanitarian relief," Motive (U.S.), XXX (Feb. 1970), 48-53.


"Aid from Norway to Nigeria - Biafra," Internasjonal Politikk (Oslo), No. 3 (1969), 436-9.
In Norwegian with English summary.


Aitken, William. "On the airstrip at Uli," Venture (July 1969), 13-16. The airstrip at Uli, a small town in Biafra, received most of the relief brought into the state from abroad by relief agencies, and its existence until its fall on Jan. 10, 1970, symbolized the Biafran resistance.


Akinyemi, A. Bolaji. "Nigeria and Fernando Po, 1958-1966; the politics of irridentism," African Affairs, LXIX (July 1970), 236-49. Portugal, sympathetic to Biafra, allowed Fernando-Po, its small colony off the Nigerian coast, to be used as an operational relief base for Biafra.
Akyea, E. O. "Biafra: the politics of relief agencies," Legon Observer, V, No. 4 (1970), 8-9.


Alima, J. B. "La Croix-Rouge paralysée," Jeune Afrique, No. 446 (July 21, 1969), 69.


"All-party plea for Biafra," Manchester Guardian, Nov. 11, 1969, p. 8. Widespread reports of starvation stirred the conscience of many members of the British Parliament who urged their Government to send more relief to Nigeria.

(STARVATION AND RELIEF)

Aluko, Samuel. "Displaced Nigerians," <u>West Africa</u>, No. 2601 (April 8, 1967), 463.
 The problem of rehabilitating Eastern Nigerians who fled other parts of Nigeria or
 lost their relatives and property.

"Anflug bei Nacht. Luftbrücke des Roten Kreuzes nach Biafra," <u>Deutsches Rotes
 Kreuz</u>, H. 11 (1968), 16-20.

Asika, Anthony Ukpabi. "Rehabilitation and resettlement," Seminar Paper, Ibadan,
 1969.

Ayandele, E. A. "The 'Humanitarian' factor in Nigerian affairs," <u>Nigerian Opinion</u>
 (Nov. 1968), 357-64.

Berge, E. "The Norwegian church relief and humanitarian relief efforts in Nigeria-
 Biafra," <u>Internasjonal Politikk</u> (Oslo), No. 3 (1969), 452-7.
 In Norwegian with English summary.

"Biafra: howling for food," <u>Newsweek,</u> (Feb. 2, 1970), 9-10.

"Biafra rejects plan to resume mercy flights," <u>L.A. Times,</u> Sept. 15, 1969, Part 1,
 p. 19.

"Biafra relief flights," <u>N.Y. Times,</u> Sept. 20, 1969, p. 28.

"Biafran child refugees," <u>Afr. Inst. Bull.</u>, (August 1969), 306-10.

"Biafran relief: both sides cite agreement on Red Cross aid formula," <u>Christian Sci.
 Mon.</u>, Sept. 10, 1969, p. 7.
 The difficulty of the International Committee of the Red Cross in finding any relief
 proposal acceptable to both sides.

"Biafrans die as politics holds up mercy flights," <u>Washington Post</u>, August 1969,
 p. A19.
 Biafra rejected any relief plan that implied its dependence on the Federal Govern-

(STARVATION AND RELIEF)

ment or prejudicial to its military position, and the Nigerian Government opposed any plan that symbolized political independence for Biafra. Thus massive relief shipments were hindered.

"Biafrans reject Red Cross accord," N.Y. Times, Sept. 15, 1969, p. 13.

"Bomber für Babys," Der Spiegel (Hamburg), No. 30 (July 22, 1968), 66-8.

Booth, A. R. "The Churches in the Nigerian war: the threat of moral imperialism," Round Table, LX (April 1970), 121-7.

"Both sides must agree," Times (London), July 10, 1969, p. 11.
An editorial on the relief negotiations between the International Committee of the Red Cross and the warring parties.

"British M.P.'s debate relief and arms," West Africa, No. 2669 (July 27, 1968), 881.

Brown, Richard E. "Mission to Biafra (Jan. 1969): a study and survey of a population under stress," Clinical Pediatrics, (Philadelphia), VIII (June 1969), 313-21.

_____ and J. Mayer. "Famine and disease in Biafra: an assessment," Trop. Geogr. Med., XXI (Sept. 1969), 348-52.
A study of starvation, malnutrition and death in the state.

Butenschon, P. "Humanitarian intervention and humanitarian foreign policy," Internasjonal Politikk (Oslo), No. 3 (1969), 377-81.
In Norwegian with English summary.

Carl, Beverly May. "American assistance to victims of the Nigeria-Biafra war: defects in the prescriptions on foreign disaster relief," Harvard Int. Law J., XII (Spring 1971), 191-259.
Emphasis is on the role of the U.S. Agency for International Development.

(STARVATION AND RELIEF)

Caudron, J. P. "L'Atroce agonie du Biafra: des centaines de milliers d'hommes ne survivent que grace à l'aide des églises," Informations Catholiques Internationales (Paris), (Jan. 1970), 4-6.

"Churchmen urge Biafra aid route," N.Y. Times, Aug. 23, 1969, p. 9.
The churchmen, however, denied any political motivations, contending that their interest was purely humanitarian.

Dale, T. "The Norwegian Red Cross and humanitarian aid in Nigeria-Biafra," Internasjonal Politikk (Oslo), No. 3 (1969), 449-51.

"Death rate from starvation is reported rising again in Biafra," N.Y. Times, Aug. 24, 1969, p. 16.

Decraene, Philippe. "Le C.I.C.R. tente vainement d'intervenir en faveur de belligérants décidés à mener une guerre totale," Le Monde, July 17, 1969, pp. pp. 1 & 8.
The political involvement of the International Committee of the Red Cross.

"Department reviews U.S. efforts to aid victims of the Nigerian civil war," U.S. Dept. State Bull., LXI (August 4, 1969), 94-100.
Statement made before the U.S. Senate Sub-Committee on the refugees.

Drew, E. B. "Reports; Washington; bungling Biafran relief," Atlantic Monthly, CXV (June 1970), 4+.
Critical of U.S. relief efforts.

Eide, A. "International law in relation to humanitarian intervention in Biafra," Internasjonal Politikk (Oslo), No. 3 (1969), 389-405.
In Norwegian with English summary.

Familusi, J. B. Nutrition and disease patterns in a war affected area of Eastern Nigeria. Ibadan: Institute of Child Health, University of Ibadan, 1969. 19 p.

(STARVATION AND RELIEF)

"Feed the starving," Times (London), July 4, 1968, p. 9.
An editorial.

Fergusson, Bernard. "A British observer's view of the Nigerian war," Times
(London), March 12, 1969, p. 11.

Feuillet, C. "Que fait la Croix-Rouge au Biafra?" Jeune Afrique (Paris), No. 443
(July 6, 1969), 28-31.

Freymond, J. "Nigéria-Biafra: l'aide aux victimes de la guerre civile," Preuves
(Paris), No. 1 (1970), 70-83.

Friendly, Alfred. "The Children are starving," New Republic, CLIX (Aug. 17, 1968),
22-6.
Suggests that Biafra should be allowed to be independent, not because the Ibos were
right in breaking away from the Federation, but because of the scope and profundity
of human suffering already generated by the war.

Gans, Bruno. "A Biafran relief mission," Lancet (March 20, 1969), 660-5.

Goodell, Charles. "Report of the Biafra study mission," Congressional Record
(Washington, D.C.) (Feb. 25, 1969).
The fact-finding mission to Nigeria, Feb. 7-12, 1969, was led by Charles Goodell,
a U.S. Senator, accompanied by Dr. Charles Dunn, his Administrative Assistant;
Dr. George Axinn, Professor of Agriculture at Michigan State University; Dr. Roy
Brown, Professor of Preventive Medicine and pediatrics at Tufts University;
George Orick, former Consultant to UNICEF and Dr. Jean Mayer, Professor of
Nutrition at Harvard University. The study mission made six specific and technical
recommendations to the Congress in their fields of professional expertise.

"Gowon's doves win and aid can restart," Observer (London), Sept. 7, 1969, p. 1.

Great Britain. Colonial Office. Nigeria. British relief advisory team, report by
Lord Hunt and Sir Colin Thornley. London: H.M.S.O., 1968. 14 p. (Cmnd. 3727).

(STARVATION AND RELIEF)

Great Britain. Colonial Office.   <u>Report of Lord Hunt.  The problem of relief in the</u>
<u>aftermath of the Nigerian civil war</u>.  London: H.M.S.O., 1970,  16 p.  (Cmnd.
4275).


Hall, Richard.  "Biafra's cowboy Catholics,"  <u>Nova</u>  (April 1970),  62-5.


Hilton, Bruce.  <u>Highly irregular</u>.  New York: Macmillan, 1969.  153 p.
The inadequacy of the Biafran relief.


Holton, Robert R.  "Missionaries doubt Nigeria would wipe out Biafra tribe,"
<u>National Catholic Reporter,</u>  V  (March 5, 1969),  3.


"A Hopeful beginning,"  <u>Times</u>  (London),  July 15, 1969,  p. 9.
An editorial on relief negotiations.


International Committee of the Red Cross.  <u>Annual report of the International Commit-</u>
<u>tee of the Red Cross</u>.  (1968).  Geneva, 1969.  103 p.
Nigeria-Biafra, pp. 9-19.


"Is starvation a legitimate weapon?"  <u>Newsweek</u>  (Sept 30, 1968),  23.


Johnson, Lyndon Baines.  "President calls on O.A.U. to break deadlock relief for
Nigeria: text of message to Organization of African Unity, Sept. 13, 1968,"  <u>U.S.</u>
<u>Dept. State Bull.</u>,  LIX  (Oct. 7, 1968),  356.
The American President believed that the eventual resolution of the Nigerian conflict should come from the Organization of African Unity, that made many fruitless
attempts to end the war.  During the meeting of the body in Sept. 1968, President
Johnson sent a special message urging the body to devise a relief plan acceptable to
both sides so that food and medicine could be sent to the victims of the war, which
had been hampered by the political intransigence of the combatants.


_____  "U.S. supports relief efforts for Nigeria: statement, together with Department
statement, July 11, 12, 1968,"  <u>U.S. Dept.  State Bull.</u>,  LIX  (July 29, 1968), 124-5.

(STARVATION AND RELIEF)

Junker, H. <u>Hinter den Fronten. Als Arzt in Biafra. Mit dem deutschen roten Kreuz im Einsatz.</u> Wurzburg: Arena, 1969. 264 p.

Katzenbach, Nicholas de. "The Tragedy of Nigeria," <u>U.S. Dept. State Bull.</u>, LIX (Dec. 23, 1968), 653-8.
The U.S. Under-Secretary of State argued that the humanitarian and political aspects of the war were deeply interwoven and restated U.S. policy.

"Lagos et l'église catholique," <u>Afrique Nouvelle</u> (Jan. 22-28, 1970), 13.
States that the Nigerian Government resents the Catholic Church because most of the unauthorized church-sponsored relief flights into Biafra were organized by the Roman Catholics.

"Leaders argue, children starve," <u>Economist</u>, CCXXVIII (July 13, 1968), 21-2.
The inability of both sides to devise any relief plan not considered prejudicial to the sovereignty of the Federal Nigeria or Biafra hindered any massive relief shipments to the secessionist state.

Lindsay, Kennedy. "Political factors in Biafran relief," <u>Venture</u> (Feb. 1970), 7-10.

"Long Beach to Biafra," <u>L.A. Times, West Magazine</u>, June 29, 1969, p. 8.
Detailed account of various relief flights from Long Beach, California to Biafra. Includes many illustrations.

"Making relief work," <u>West Africa</u>, No. 2716 (June 21, 1969), 697-8.

Mathiesen, H. "The Humanitarian relief effort-status," <u>Internasjonal Politikk</u> (Oslo), No. 3 (1969), 440-8.
In Norwegian with English summary.

Mohr, Charles. "Rogers (U.S. Secretary of State) seeks to assure Lagos U.S. respects the relief plans," <u>N.Y. Times</u>, Feb. 20, 1970, p. 2.
Guarantee by the U.S. Government not to fly relief supplies into former Biafra without the authorization of the Nigerian Government.

(STARVATION AND RELIEF)


Mok, Michael. "Death rattle of an encircled nation," <u>Life,</u> XLIX, No. 5 (1968), 24-9.
The rise of death rate in Biafra.


Moore, C. Robert. "International relief efforts in Nigeria," <u>U.S. Dept. State Bull.</u>, LIX (Nov. 4, 1968), 484-6.
The author was at the time U.S. Deputy Assistant Secretary of State for African Affairs.


Newson, D. D. and C. C. Ferguson. "Relief and rehabilitation in Nigeria: statements, Jan. 21, 1970," <u>U.S. Dept. State Bull.</u>, LXII (Feb. 16, 1970), 185-8.
C. C. Ferguson, Professor of Law at Howard University and later appointed U.S. Ambassador to Uganda, was President Nixon's Special Relief Coordinator for Nigeria during the war.


"Nigeria disputes with Red Cross," <u>Afr. Res. Bull.</u>, VI (July 15, 1969), 1442-4.
The International Red Cross and other national Red Cross Societies found it very difficult to formulate any relief proposals acceptable to both sides.


"Nigeria move signals tougher Biafra policy," <u>Christian Sci. Mon.</u>, July 3, 1969, p. 6.
The tightening of the Federal blockade, air and sea, and warning to relief agencies not to make any unauthorized relief flights into the secessionist state.


"Nigeria - end of civil war, British relief aid," <u>Survey Brit. Comm. Affairs,</u> IV, No. 5 (Feb. 1970), 195-200.


"Nigerians pour in relief for Ibos," <u>Observer</u> (London), Jan. 18, 1970, p. 1.
Relief shipments into former Biafra by the Federal Government on the Biafran surrender to the Federal forces on Jan. 12, 1970.


Nixon, Richard. "Special U.S. Coordinator appointed for Nigerian relief efforts," <u>U.S. Dept. State Bull.</u>, LXX (March 17, 1969), 222-3.
Professor Clarence Ferguson of the Howard University School of Law was appointed by President Nixon on Feb. 1969, as his Special Relief Coordinator.

(STARVATION AND RELIEF)

"No food, no guns," Economist, CCXXXII (July 5, 1969), 14-15.
Acute shortage of food and weapons to continue the war in Biafra.

Norbye, O. D. K. "Emergency relief and development aid," Internasjonal Politikk
(Oslo), No. 3 (1969), 382-8.
In Norwegian with English summary.

Olsen, C. "Deux équipes de voluntaires danois sont partis pour le Biafra," Le
Monde, Aug. 13, 1968, p. 4.
The Danish relief for Biafra.

_____ "Les Pays scandinaves et Biafra," Rev. Fr. Etud. Pol. Afr., LII (1970),
77-111.
Review of the role of the Scandinavian countries in the Biafran relief.

"Ottawa told to aid the dying, then worry about Nigeria," Globe and Mail (Canada),
Aug. 30, 1969, pp. 1 & 4.
The Canadian Government urged to help feed the starving in Biafra first and then
consider the question of Nigerian unity, which was main reason for the declaration
of the war.

Pélissier, René. "Sao Tome: Outpost of Portuguese colonialism and lifeline to
Biafra," Africa Report, XV (Jan. 1970), 27.
Portugal, believed to be sympathetic to the secessionists, allowed its colony, Sao
Tome, an island off the coast of West Africa to be used as an operational relief
base for Biafra.

"A Policy of famine," Times (London), June 28, 1969, p. 8.
An editorial critical of British inadequate relief efforts, arguing that the starvation
bordered on genocide.

"Policy of famine in Nigeria: a time for world action," Times (London), July 1, 1969,
p. 9.
Letters to the editor with opposing viewpoints on relief.

(STARVATION AND RELIEF)

"Policy on Nigeria/Biafra: Congress, public press for more Biafran relief,"
  Congressional Quarterly, Weekly Report, XXVII (April 4, 1969),   481-4.
  One of the most informative articles on the war, analyzing official U.S. position on
  the conflict, attitudes of the Congress; the motivations of the major relief organizations which sprang up throughout the United States.

"The Politics of relief," Motive (U.S.), (Feb. 1970).

"Red Cross in the field," West Africa, No. 2748 (Jan. 31, 1970), 127-8.
  The activities of the Nigerian Red Cross in former Biafra.

"Red Cross in trouble," West Africa, No. 2716 (June 21, 1969), 698-9.
  The plane of the International Red Cross Society was shot down for violating the
  Nigerian air space.

"Red Cross leaving Nigeria," Times (London), Oct. 3, 1969, p. 8.
  The inability of the International Committee of the Red Cross to devise relief plans
  acceptable to both sides in the conflict.

Reed, David. "A Nation is dying," Readers Digest, (March 1969), 75-80.
  High death toll in Biafra through starvation.

"Relief needed for another year?" West Africa, No. 2774 (Aug. 8, 1970), 890-2.
  The economic situation in former Biafra still deplorable.

"Relief plan spurned by Biafra," Washington Post, Sept. 15, 1969, Section A, p. 1.

"Rettung durch die Stockfisch Bomber," Der Spiegel (Hamburg), No. 24 (June 9,
  1969), 106-14; No. 25 (June 16, 1969), 104-16.

"Roadblock: solution to Nigerian relief problem eludes efforts of Nixon's coordinator,"
  Christian Sci. Mon., Oct. 2, 1969, p. 1.
  Professor Clarence Ferguson unable to formulate any relief plan agreeable to both
  sides.

Rogers, William G. "A Post-mortem on Biafra needed: a (United States) disaster
  relief unit," Ripon Forum, VII (May 1971), 13-21.

(STARVATION AND RELIEF)

Rosemann, H. <u>Heidelberg hilft Biafra</u>. Heidelberg, 1969. 190 p.

Sandegren, K. "On international humanitarian relief in civil wars," <u>Internasjonal Politikk</u> (Oslo), No. 3 (1969), 310-12.

Sargos, P. "Médecin au Biafra," <u>Esprit</u> (Feb. 1970), 371-80.

Schwarz, Walter. "Mr. Wilson and Biafran starvation," <u>Manchester Guardian</u>, Sept. 22, 1969, p. 8.
Attitude of Harold Wilson, Britain's Prime Minister, to the relief plans for Biafra, which rejected the daylight relief flights supported by Wilson.

Shepherd, G. W. "Biafra - the politics of saving lives," <u>Africa Today</u>, XV, No. 4 (1968), 1-2.

"The Situation in Nigeria," <u>Survey Brit. Comm. Affairs</u>, III (Aug. 1969), 700-9.
Review of the British medical aid.

Smock, Audrey Chapman. "The Politics of relief," <u>Africa Report</u>, XV (Jan. 1970), 24-6.
Critical examination of the activities and problems of various relief agencies and the political implications of relief in general.

Stacey, N. "Must Biafra starve?" <u>Spectator</u> (London), No. 7307 (July 12, 1968), 44-5.

"Starvation as a weapon," <u>Christian Sci. Mon.</u>, July 3, 1969, p. 20.
Questions the morality of using starvation as a military weapon.

Stokke, O. "Foreign policy effects of governmental humanitarian intervention in Nigeria-Biafra," <u>Internasjonal Politikk</u> (Oslo), No. 3 (1969), 415-35.
In Norwegian with English summary.

(STARVATION AND RELIEF)

Sullivan, John R. <u>Breadless Biafra</u>. Dayton, Ohio: Pflaum, 1969. 104 p.
An eye-witness account of starvation in Biafra by reporter for the U.S. National
Catholic News Service.

U.S. Congress. House. Committee on Foreign Affairs. <u>Report of the Special fact-</u>
<u>finding mission to Nigeria, Feb. 7-20, 1969, by Hon. Charles C. Diggs, Jr.,</u>
<u>Michigan, Chairman and Hon. J. Herbert Burke, Florida, pursuant to H. Res. 143.</u>
Washington, D.C., 1969. 59 p. (91st Congress, 1st session.)
The Report is critical of the Biafran leadership for not allowing the use of land
corridor for relief supplies and warned against any U.S. military intervention in
the civil war.

_____ <u>Report of the Special Coordinator for Nigerian relief; hearing, April 24, 1969.</u>
Washington, D.C., 1969. 23 p. (91st Congress, 1st session.)
Report of Professor Clarence Ferguson after his visit to Federal Nigeria and
Biafra. He realized that the political and humanitarian aspects of the war were
deeply interwoven, as he could not get both sides to accept his relief plans.

U.S. Congress. Senate. Committee on Foreign Relations. Sub-Committee on African
Affairs. <u>Nigerian-Biafran relief situation; hearing, Oct. 4, 1968.</u> Washington,
D.C., 1968. 89 p. (90th Congress, 2nd session.)

U.S. Congress. Senate. Committee on the Judiciary. Sub-Committee to investigate
problems connected with refugees and escapees. <u>Relief problems in Nigeria-Biafra;</u>
<u>hearings, pts. 1-2, July 15, 1969 - January 22, 1970.</u> Washington, D.C., 1969-70.
2 pts. 291 p. (91st Congress, 1st and 2nd sessions.)

"U.S. planes available to assist relief efforts in Nigeria: Department announcement,
December 27, with statement December 31, 1968." <u>U.S. Dept. State Bull.</u>, LX
(Jan. 13, 1969), 30-1.

"U.S. pledges additional $ 6 million to I.C.R.C. for Nigerian relief," <u>U.S. Dept.</u>
<u>State Bull.</u>, LX (March 31, 1969), 281.
I.C.R.C. is the International Committee of the Red Cross.

"What hope for relief?" <u>West Africa.</u>, No. 2667 (July 13, 1968), 798-9.

PEACE EFFORTS

"The Aburi Agreements," <u>Nigerian Opinion</u>, III, No. 1 (1967), 1-2.
The most important meeting of the Nigerian military leaders before the Biafran secession was held in Aburi, Ghana, on Jan. 4-5, 1967, during which a new political and constitutional system for Nigeria was formulated, rioting in Northern Nigeria and refuge problems in Eastern Nigeria discussed and decisions made. These decisions were later differently interpreted by both Federal and Eastern Nigerian authorities, and this led to the secession of Eastern Nigeria and Civil War.

<u>Aburi Meeting of Nigerian Military Leaders, 4th & 5th January 1967 (as recorded by the Ghana Government and released by command of Lt. Col. Odumegwu Ojukwu, Military Governor of Eastern Nigeria)</u>. Enugu: Phonodisc, 1967. 24 slides, 12 discs.

"L'Action de Paul pour la paix au Nigéria depuis l'origine du drame," <u>Afrique Nouvelle</u>, (Feb. 19-25, 1970), 12.
Pope Paul's peace initiatives to end the war were abortive.

Adeyemi, I. "Une Mission secrète d'Azikiwe à Paris," <u>Afrique Actuelle</u> (Sept. 1968), 2-3.

Bernetel, P. "En deçà de la négociation," <u>Jeune Afrique</u>, No. 440 (June 15, 1969), 21-3.

_____ "Nigeria: entre la guerre et la paix," <u>Jeune Afrique</u>, No. 474 (Feb. 3, 1970), 12-13.

"Biafra sovereignty demand checks hope of peace," <u>Times</u> (London), Dec. 13, 1968, p. 1.
Biafra's insistence on absolute independence rather than some degree of local autonomy within a united Nigeria considered the greatest obstacle to any serious peace negotiations.

"Biafran offer to end secession reported," <u>N.Y. Times</u>, Nov. 4, 1969, p. 2.
The rumor that Biafra would agree to the re-unification of the country provided that it was given considerable local autonomy was dismissed by the Biafran Government

(PEACE EFFORTS)


as "ridiculous."


Brockway, F. "Our Nigerian peace mission," <u>New Statesman</u>, (Jan. 3, 1969), 7.
The British peace mission to Nigeria.


Cervenka, Zdenek. <u>The Organization of African Unity and its charter</u>. 2nd ed., New
York: Praeger, 1969. 253 p.
Includes attitudes of various African states to the war based upon the provisions of
the body's charter.
Rev: <u>Choice</u>, VII (March 1970), 150.
<u>Library J.</u>, XCV (Jan. 1, 1970), 74.
_____ <u>Peace-keeping machinery in Africa - lessons out of Nigerian war</u>. Uppsala:
Scandinavian Institute of African Studies, 1970. 15 p.


Cheshire, Leonard. "Why peace mission failed," <u>Manchester Guardian,</u> Nov. 22,
1969, p. 8.
The fruitlessness of the peace efforts of the British Prime Minister, Harold Wilson,
during his visit to Nigeria in March 1969.


"The Conditions of peace," <u>Nigerian Opinion</u>, III, Nos. 8-9 (1967), 1.


De St. Jorre, John. "Wilson makes no headway in Lagos talks," <u>Observer</u> (London),
March 30, 1969, p. 4.


"Dr, Azikiwe peace plan," <u>Africa Digest</u>, XVI (April 1969), 23-4.
The peace plan of former President of Nigeria at Oxford on February 17, 1969,
called for an international action of the Security Council of the Nations initiated by
the United States to end the war. This proposal was rejected by the Nigerian
Government on the ground that it was outside the jurisdiction of the U.N., and
besides such an action could constitute an interference in the internal affairs of
Nigeria.


Elias, Taslim Olawale. "The Commission of mediation, conciliation and arbitration
of the Organization of African Unity," <u>British Yearbook of International Law</u>, 1964,
pp. 336-54.

(PEACE EFFORTS)

Dr. Elias, the most distinguished Africal legal scholar, has served as Dean of the Faculty of Law, University of Lagos, and Federal Attorney-General of Nigeria. Author of numerous books, he is an international figure in international and constitutional laws.

"Enahoro's middle ways," West Africa, No. 2755 (March 28, 1970), 325-7.
   Chief Anthony Enahoro, Nigeria's Commissioner for Information and Labour, leader of peace delegation to peace talks with Biafra, said, before the Nigerian Society of International Law, that Nigeria would follow a non-alignment foreign policy.

"Ending a war," Africa Digest, XVI (April 1969), 21-3.
   The irreconcilable goals of the combatants; British and French interests; attitudes of other Africans; and relief organizations.

Fajuyi, F. A. Towards peace in Western Nigeria; a statement by Lt. Col. F. A. Fajuyi on his assumption of office of the Military Governor of Western Region on Jan. 21, 1966. Ibadan: Ministry of Information, 1966. 2 p.
   The author died in the Nigerian second military coup.

Gavin, R. J. "A Time to talk," Nigerian Opinion, (Oct. 1967), 252-4.

Gowon, Yakubu. Four steps to national stability; broadcast on the 1968-69. Lagos: Federal Ministry of Information, 1968. 15 p.

_____ Let us reconcile. Broadcast - on January, 1970, following formal surrender by the rebels. Apapa, Nigeria, 1970. 15 p.
   The acceptance of the Biafran surrender in Jan. 1970, by the Head of Nigerian Military Government.

Gowon's spotlight on the future of the Ibos. Lagos: Federal Ministry of Information, 1967. 6 p.
   Text of an interview held in Oct. 24, 1967. The Nigerian leader states that the Ibos would be reintegrated into the country without punishment and participate like other Nigerians in rebuilding the country.

Horgan, John. "Coexistence in Nigeria," Commonweal, LXXXVIII (May 3, 1968), 203-5.

(PEACE EFFORTS)

Hornby, R. "Search for peace in Nigeria," Round Table, LX (Jan. 1970), 34-8.

"How to end the Nigerian war," Washington Post, Nov. 12, 1969, p. A 22.
An editorial urging the Nigerian Federal Government to accept peace negotiations with Biafra without pre-conditions.

"Is Biafra ready for peace?" Economist, (Nov. 8, 1969), 31.

"Is peace possible?" West Africa, No. 2624 (Sept. 16, 1967), 1193-4.

"Is there a basis for peace in Nigeria?" Africa and the World (Feb. 1968), 3-4; 30-1.

"Is there a middle way?" West Africa, No. 2715 (June 14, 1969), 667.

Kahn, Cynthia. "The O.A.U. hurrying nowhere," Africa Today, (Oct./Nov. 1968), 1-2.
Reviews critically the efforts made by the Organization of African Unity to effect a negotiated settlement to the war, noting that the impotence of the body was due to the provisions of its charter and lack of independent thinking among African leaders.

"Lagos rejects Azikiwe's plan," Times (London), Feb. 18, 1969, p. 7.
The plan which called for an international action to end the war suggested use of plebiscite to decide on the reunification of Nigeria under the United Nations supervision.

Leapman, Michael. "Biafra: the best hope for peace," New Statesman, LXXVI (Dec. 6, 1968), 775-6.

Legum, Colin. "Breaking the Nigeria-Biafra deadlock," America, CXX (May 24, 1969), 623-7.

_____ "New hope for Nigeria: the search for national unity," Round Table (April

(PEACE EFFORTS)

1968),  127-36.


Legum, Colin.  "The Path to peace,"  <u>Help</u>  (April 1969),  41-3.


_____  "The Way out of the Biafran tragedy,"  <u>War/Peace Report</u>,  IX  (March 1969),
5-7.


Lindsay, Kennedy.  "Can there be a peace settlement in Nigeria?"  <u>Africa Report</u>,
(Jan. 1970),  14-15.
Examines the minority problems and their impact on the conflict and gives concrete
proposals for a political settlement of the war.  Dr. Lindsay is former Professor of
History, University of Nigeria.


Martel, P. A.  "Nigeria-Biafra rendez-vous à Addis Ababa,"  <u>Jeune Afrique</u>,  No.
396 (August 11, 1968),  32-3.
A peace talk at Addis Ababa, Ethiopia, headquarters of the Organization of African
Unity, was fruitless.


_____  "La Porte entreouverte,"  <u>Jeune Afrique</u>,  No. 397  (Aug. 18, 1968),  22-3.


Mckenna, John.  "Elements of Nigerian peace,"  <u>Foreign Affairs</u>,  XLVII  (July 1969),
668-91.
The secession was caused by lack of security among the Ibos after the 1966 rioting in
Northern Nigeria; the Federal Government declared war to preserve Nigeria's
political and economic integrity.


Meisler, Stanley.  "African summit talks close in futile pomp,"  <u>L.A. Times</u>,  Sept.
17, 1968,  Part 1, p. 16.
Critical of the inability of the Organization of African Unity to end the war, suggesting that the meeting of the African leaders is only an opportunity to display flowery
military apparel.  The author is an American journalist, African Correspondent for
the <u>Los Angeles Times</u>.


Nagel, R. and R. Rathbone.  "The O.A.U. at Kinshasa,"  <u>World Today</u>,  XXIII  (Nov.

(PEACE EFFORTS)


1967), 473-83.
The main reason for the meeting of the Organization of African Unity is Nigerian
Civil War. Kinshasa is the Capital of Zaire.


Nigeria. Ending the fighting; broadcast to the nation by His Excellency Major-General
Yakubu Gowon. Lagos, 1968? 10 p.
Although General Gowon preferred "a negotiated settlement to the harsh alternative
of a total military victory," he firmly reiterated his two basic conditions of peace:
"The rebels must acknowledge that Nigeria remains One united nation; and second,
they accept the new structure of twelve equal states in the Federation."


_____ Gowon's spotlight on the future of the Ibos. Lagos, 1967. 6 p.


_____ Report on the O.A.U. Consultative Mission to Nigeria. Apapa: Nigerian
National Press, 1968? 36 p.
The four man peace delegation was an outcome of the fourth summit meeting of the
Organization of African Unity held in September 1967, and comprised the following
Heads of State: Emperor Haile Selassie of Ethiopia; President Hamani Diori of
Niger Republic; President Ahidjo of Cameroun; Lt. General Ankra of Ghana.
Includes the text of Gowon's address to the Consultative Mission, specifying two
conditions for peace: Biafran renunciation of secession and acceptance of the 12
state structure, and the text of the address of Haile Selassie in reply to Gowon's
welcome address.


_____ Victory for unity. Apapa: Nigerian National Press, 1970. 12 p.
Speeches of Major-General Phillip Effiong, Deputy Biafran leader, calling for an
armistice, and of Major-General Gowon, accepting the request - the surrender -
on January 12, 1970.


Nigeria. Embassy. The Dawn of lasting peace; address by Major-General Yakubu
Gowon. Washington, D.C., 1968.


_____ Nigeria: peace talks and relief assistance. Washington, D.C., 1968.


Nigeria. Federal Ministry of Information. The Collapse of rebellion and prospects of

(PEACE EFFORTS)


lasting peace. Lagos, 1967.
The secession was crushed only three years later on January 12, 1970.


_____ Enough is enough: a challenging appeal to the Ibos of Nigeria. Lagos, 1967. 16p.


_____ Federal peace efforts. Lagos, 1968. 15 p.
Gives background account of the war and recounts various peace overtures made
by the Federal Government at Aburi, Ghana, and the meeting of the Organization
of African Unity at Niamey, Niger, and Addis Ababa, Ethiopia; the Federal relief
proposals, especially land and air corridor flights by daylight into Biafra.


_____ Framework for settlement: the Federal case in Kampala. Lagos, 1968. 18 p.
The Chief Federal peace delegate to talks with Biafra in Kampala, Uganda, Chief
Anthony Enahoro, outlines the Federal twelve-point proposal based upon the
principle of a united Nigeria.


_____ Operation reconstruction. Policies and objectives as outlined in public speeches
by His Excellency, Lt. Col. Yakubu Gowon. Lagos, 1966. 30 p.


_____ Peace, stability and harmony in post-war Nigeria. Lagos, 1968. 10 p.
Gowon's address to World Press on Jan. 5, 1968.


_____ Zik in Lagos. Lagos, 1969. 11 p.
The dramatic appearance in Lagos of Dr. Nnamdi Azikiwe, an Ibo and former
President of Nigeria, raised a great speculation in international circles that a
compromise solution to the conflict might be at hand. Until then a Biafran supporter,
immediately he returned to London where he had been living for several months, he
renounced his support of Biafra and called a general amnesty for Biafrans, whom
he requested to give up their bid for independence and seek accommodation with
the Federal Government.


Nigeria. Military Leaders' Meeting, Aburi, Ghana, 1967. [Report of] the meeting of
the military leaders held at Peduase Lodge...4th and 5th January, 1967. Lagos:
Federal Ministry of Information, Printing Division, 1967. 105 p.
A very important document - report of the historic meeting of Nigerian leaders in

(PEACE EFFORTS)

Aburi, Ghana, to decide on the future of Nigeria following the rioting, killings of Ibos in Northern Nigeria and Ibo mass exodus to the East. The subsequent differing interpretations of the Aburi agreements spelled the doom of the nation and hastened the Civil War.

Nigeria. State House. Ad hoc conference on constitutional proposals, Lagos, 1966. Memoranda submitted by the delegations. Lagos, 1967. 182 p.

Nigeria, Western. Ministry of Home Affairs and Information. Yoruba peace recipes: Nigerian situation - Dec. 1966. Ibadan, 1966?

"Nigeria - abortive peace talks," Afr. Res. Bull., VI, No. 12 (1970), 1613-5.

"Nigeria. A chink of light," Economist, (Jan. 11, 1969), 18-31.

"Nigeria -Biafra - première table ronde," Evénement (Paris), No. 35 (Jan. 1969), 13-19.

"Nigeria - external initiatives," Afr. Res. Bull., VI, No. 3 (1969), 1351-3.

"Nigeria: further peace moves fail," Afr. Res. Bull., V, (July 15, 1968), 1095-9.

"Nigeria - General Ojukwu's proposals," Afr. Res. Bull., VI, No. 11 (1969), 1586-9.

"Nigeria - la guerre doit cesser, la paix est possible, l'opinion africaine peut et doit agir," Jeune Afrique, No. 3439 (June 8, 1969), 14-17.

"Nigeria - peace talks fail," Afr. Res. Bull., V, No. 5 (1968), 1068-74.

"Nigeria - statement on Aburi Agreement," Afr. Res. Bull., IV, No. 2 (1967), 717.

(PEACE EFFORTS)

"Nigeria - Supreme Council Meeting," Afr. Res. Bull., IV, No. 1 (1967), 698-9.

"Nigeria's priorities of victory," Manchester Guardian, Jan. 17, 1970, p. 1.
An editorial.

Offroy, Raymond. "Une Négociation est maintenant possible au Biafra," Le Figaro,
July 14, 1969, p. 4.
The author is former French Ambassador to Nigeria.

Ojukwu, Chukwuemeka Odumegwu. As we go to Kampala. Enugu: Ministry of Information, 1968. 12 p.
Speech delivered by Ojukwu to his people on May 19, 1968, on the prospects of peace
negotiations to be held on May 23, 1968, in Kampala, Uganda.

_____ "Nous voulons négocier. Mais nous n'abandonnerons rien," Jeune Afrique,
No. 3439 (June 8, 1969), 24-5.

Okpaku, Joseph. "Nigeria today, the dilemma of peace," In Joseph Okpaku, ed.
Nigeria: dilemma of nationhood; an analysis of the Nigeria-Biafra conflict by
Nigerian scholars. New York: The Third Press, 1972, pp. 366-78.

"Paix au Nigéria," Eglise Vivante (Paris), XX, No. 2 (1968), 126-8.

"Peace plan for Nigeria by Azikiwe," Times (London), Feb. 17, 1969, p. 4.
The four point peace proposal made at Rhodes House, Oxford, was rejected by the
Nigerian Government on the ground that it presumed Biafra a legally independent
state and challenged Nigeria's territorial integrity.

"Pope presses Biafrans on peace," N.Y. Times, August 3, 1969, p. 46.
Pope Paul VI generally regarded as sympathetic to the Biafrans made an unsuccessful effort to end the war by holding an interview with the Biafran and Federal
peace delegates separately on August 1, 1969, in Kampala, Uganda, where he was to
consecrate African Bishops.

(PEACE EFFORTS)

"Prospects for peace; Kampala and after," Ibadan (Feb. 1969), 3-5.

"Radio says Nigeria bars truce offer," N.Y. Times, July 20, 1969, p. 2.

"La Réconciliation au Nigeria n'a pas d'Ojukwu," Afrique Nouvelle (April 15-21, 1971), 6.
At the news conference with General Gowon during his visit to Northern Cameroons on April 7, 1971, the Nigerian leader specified his domestic and foreign policies. He rejected the view that total reconciliation was impossible in Nigeria without the return of former Biafran leader now in exile. On the Soviet support of Nigerian effort to crush the secession, he noted, "Our relations with the Soviet Union are based upon the principle of mutual respect. No one can impose any ideology on us; we have our own interests and ideology which is Nigerian and African."

Report on the O.A.U. Consultative mission to Nigeria. Lagos: Federal Ministry of Information, 1967. 36 p.
In English and French.

Rulli, Giovanni. "Per la pace in Nigeria," La Civilta Cattolica, CXIX (April 6, 1968), 88-92.
Report on Biafran relief by one of the major relief agencies, Caritas Internationalis, based in Rome.

Sadler, J. R. "West Africa: searches for stability," Military Review, XLIX (Nov. 1969), 28-38.

Sapieha, L. "Healing the scars in Nigeria," Tablet, CCXXIV (May 16, 1970), 470-1.
Reintegration of the Ibos; national reconciliation and economic reconstruction.

Senghor, Léopold Sédar. "Si on veut la paix au Nigéria," Jeune Afrique (Dec. 1968), 24-5.
The author is President of Senegal.

(PEACE EFFORTS)

"Setbacks to peace in Nigeria," <u>N.Y. Times</u>, Sept. 16, 1969, p. 40.

"Towards Nigerian reconciliation," <u>Manchester Guardian</u>, Feb. 21, 1970, p. 12.
Appeals to the Nigerian Government not to take any reprisals against the former secessionists and to all Nigerians for co-operation in the national reconstruction.

Uwechue, Raph. "Biafra: a middle way to peace," <u>Observer</u> (London), Sept., 14, 1969, p. 10.
The former Biafran envoy in Paris calls for a return to the Aburi Agreements of January 1967, and pleads with both sides to be less intransigent in their demands and accept a confederal system of government within a united Nigeria. A dramatic switch from his support of total independence for Biafra to a compromise solution.

_____ "Des Concessions réciproques pour une paix juste et durable," <u>Rev. Fr. Etud. Pol. Afr.</u>, XXXV, No. 5 (1970), 517-46.

Viratelle, G. "Les Relatifs succès de la conférence d'Algier sont le fait de laborieux compromis," <u>Le Monde</u> (Daily edition), Sept. 18, 1968, p. 6.

"What happened at Niamey?" <u>West Africa</u>, No. 2669 (July 27, 1968), 854-5.
On July 20, 1968, the Biafran and Federal delegations in Niamey, Niger, during the meeting of the Organization of African Unity arranged for a formal peace talk at Addis Ababa which was held in August 1968, without results.

"Winning Nigeria's peace," <u>West Africa</u>, No. 2703 (March 22, 1969), 317-8.

# Nigerian Civil War: An Annotated Bibliography

## MILITARY OPERATIONS AND THE AFTERMATH

Adebanjo, T. "Beyond the conflict," Africa Report, XIII (June 1968), 12-15.
First Secretary of the Nigerian Embassy in the U.S.A. Examines the 12 state
structure, Federal war policy, minority issue, and the future of the country.
"The Agony of Biafra," Africa and the World, (June 1968), 3-6.

Allaun, Frank. "Your bullet?" Help (April 1969), 38-9.

Aluko, Olajide. "The Civil War and the Nigerian foreign policy," Political Quarterly,
XLII (April/June 1971), 171-90.

Anafulu, Joseph C. "An African experience: the role of a specialized library in a war
situation," Special Libraries, LXII (Jan. 1971), 32-40.
Examines the informational role of the Biafran Directorate for Propaganda Library.
Includes the subject headings and classification scheme used by the library. The
author is the Africana Librarian, University of Nigeria, Nsukka.

_____ "Reflection on the Nigerian Civil War," Ikenga (Nsukka), I (Jan. 1972),
118-20.
Review of Reflections on the Nigerian Civil War: a call to realism (1969) written
by Raph Uwechue, former Biafran Ambassador to Paris. Uwechue calls for a
compromise solution to the conflict, urging the Nigerian leaders to implement the
Aburi Accord of January 4-5, 1967, providing for a confederal system of government within a united Nigeria.

"Après l'épreuve du sang, perspectives d'une co-existence," Jeune Afrique (Paris)
(April 23, 1967), 34-61.

Arikpo, Okoi. Nigeria's post-war policy on Africa, news from Nigeria. Washington,
D.C., Embassy of Nigeria, 1970.

Armah, Ayi Kwei. "Pour les Ibos, le régime de la haine silencieuse," Jeune Afrique,
No. 355 (Oct. 29, 1967), 18-20.
The Ghanaian novelist surveys the events that led to the secession and the military
situation.

# Nigerian Civil War: An Annotated Bibliography

(MILITARY OPERATIONS AND THE AFTERMATH)

Armah, Ayi Kwei. "La Siège d'Enugu," <u>Jeune Afrique</u>, No. 354 (1967), 10.
Enugu was the original Capital of Biafra. It fell to the Federal forces on October 4, 1968, and is currently the Capital of East Central State.

"Armed robbery; Nigeria's fastest growing industry," <u>Drum Magazine</u> (Nigerian edition), No. 242 (June 1971), 2-4.
One of the main consequences of the war is a high rate of armed robbery caused by unemployment and many guns left lying around.

Asiodu, P. C. "Challenge of post-war development and reconstruction," <u>Management in Nigeria</u> (Jan. 1970), 127-44.

_____ <u>The Future of the Federal and State civil services in the context of twelve state structure.</u> Benin City: Midwest Newspapers Corp., 1971. 28 p.

Atimomo, Emiko. "The Problem of integration in post-war Nigeria," <u>Fume</u> (Benin) (1969), 51-6.

Awa, Eme. "Foundations for political reconstruction in Nigeria," <u>Ikenga</u> (Nsukka), I (Jan. 1972), 58-72.
"In this paper, we want to indicate the general nature of the conditions which can lead to the development of healthier politics than what we had known in the past and to underline the basic political structures which we must have." The author is Professor of Political Science and Dean of the Faculty of Social Studies, University of Nigeria, Nsukka.

Ayida, A.A. and H.M.A. Onitiri, eds. <u>Reconstruction and development in Nigeria:</u> <u>proceedings of a national conference, March 1969.</u> London: Oxford University Press for the Nigerian Institute of Social and Economic Research, 1971. 768 p.
Rev: <u>African Affairs,</u> LXXII (April 1973), 208-9.

Azikiwe, Nnamdi. <u>Address to officers and men of the 10th battalion and school of infantry, Biafra Army.</u> Enugu: Ministry of Information, 1967? 4 p.

Bankole, E. Bejide. "You and the Association - address to Annual General Meeting," <u>Nigerian Libraries,</u> IV (Dec. 1968), 83-6.
This address made to the Nigerian Library Association reviews the effects of the Civil War on the Association and libraries in general and calls upon its members to enhance its prestige by meeting the professional and intellectual standards expected of them.

(MILITARY OPERATIONS AND THE AFTERMATH)

Beichman, A. "Nigeria, première puissance militaire," Jeune Afrique, No. 483 (1970), 24-5.

_____ "The Political fact of Nigeria's Army," International Herald Tribune (Paris), March 20, 1970.

"Le Biafra a été vaincu," Afrique Nouvelle (Jan. 15-21, 1970), 6.
The fall of Biafra on Jan. 12, 1970 and its repercussions.

"Biafra: end of a lost cause," Newsweek, LXXV (Jan. 26, 1970), 48-50.
Biafra's surrender on January 12, 1970, put an end to its bid for independence proclaimed on May 30, 1967.

"Biafra: How to build an instant air force, the use of Swedish single-engine aircraft, MFI-9B," Time, XCIII (June 6, 1969), 38.
The air force created with the aid of the celebrated but quixotic Swedish pilot, Carl Gustav von Rosen, was a significant psychological boost to the Biafrans, though incomparably inferior to that of the Federal Government.

"Biafra: Lebendig begraben," Der Spiegel, No. 27 (Jan. 22, 1968), 70-6.

"Le Biafra n'existe plus," Afrique Nouvelle (Jan. 22-28, 1970), 6.
The defeat of Biafra means its dissolution into East Central State, Rivers State and South-East State in accordance with the Federal decree of May 27, 1967.

"Biafra: Todesurteil für ein Volk," Der Spiegel (Aug. 19, 1968), 71-6.
Relief efforts; military potentialities of both sides; interviews with opposing leaders. Numerous photographs.

"Biafrans lose their struggle," Senior Scholastic, XCVI (Feb. 2, 1970), 15-6.

"Biafra's prisoners," Times (London), June 5, 1969, p. 11.

(MILITARY OPERATIONS AND THE AFTERMATH)

An editorial on the 18 oil men working with the Italian petroleum company, AGIP, who were captured by the Biafran forces. The death sentence passed on them was later commuted by the Biafran leader, yielding to international plea for mercy.

Borders, William. "Ibos live in Enugu offices awaiting old employers," N.Y. Times, April 24, 1970, p. 2.
Resettlement of displaced workers after the war in the Capital of East Central State.

_____ "In former Biafra; the scars of war fade," N.Y. Times, Jan. 17, 1971, pp. 1 & 20.
Observes that the economic recovery of the people of the East Central State has been remarkably quick.

_____ "Nigeria, independent a decade, shows signs of living up to hopes," N.Y. Times, Oct. 1, 1970, p. 3.
Optimistic assessment of the future of Nigeria on the tenth anniversary of its independence, despite the civil war.

_____ "Nigeria prosperous again," N.Y. Times, Jan. 29, 1971, p. 49.
Quick economic recovery.

Bourjailly, Vance. "An Epitaph for Biafra," N.Y. Times Magazine (Jan. 25, 1970), 32-3; 85-7.
Reviews the circumstances of the secessionists' defeat and pays tribute to their courage, endurance and idealism. The author is a noted American novelist.

Chaliand, C. "Génocide au Nigéria," Evénement (Paris), No. 25 (Feb. 1968), 48-57.

Chapman, Audrey R. "The Civil war in Nigeria," Midstream, XIV (Jan. 1968), 12-25.

Chauleur, Pierre. "L'Agonie du Biafra," Etudes (March 1970), 325-42.

(MILITARY OPERATIONS AND THE AFTERMATH)

Chauleur, Pierre. "L'Assassinat du Biafra," Etudes (May 1968), 632–49.


Chauvel, J. F. "L'Atroce guerre du Biafra," Cri du Monde (Paris), No. 22 (1968), 10–12.


Cheiminski, R. "Biafra: the scramble for life in a dead country," Life, LXVIII (Jan. 30, 1970), 32–5.
Includes many illustrations.


Churchill, Winston. "A Time for magnanimity." Times (London), Jan. 12, 1970, p. 9.
Suggests that the Nigerian Government should not resort to any reprisals against former secessionists.


Clifford, Miles. "Nigeria on the road back," Daily Telegraph, Nov. 5, 1971, p. 14.


Colvin, Ian. "Gowon's battle with chaos," Daily Telegraph, April 16, 1971, p. 16.
Examines the magnitude of reconstruction work to be done.


Comte, G. "Biafra: l'agonie et les chances de la guerilla," Rev. Fr. Etud. Pol. Afr., No. 34 (Oct. 1968), 12–15.


Connett, Paul. "Life behind the battle," Spectator (May 9, 1969), 609–10.
Description of the daily life in the secessionist state by the President of the American Committee to Keep Biafra Alive.


"Conquest of Biafra," Round Table, LX (April 1970), 117–20.
The political implications of the Biafran defeat.


"Conversations in Biafra," Sunday Times (London), July 27, 1969, p. 13.
Life in the state and grim determination of the Ibos to fight to the end.

(MILITARY OPERATIONS AND THE AFTERMATH)

Cronje, Suzanne. "Why Biafra lost the war: Count von Rosen's theory," Times (London), Feb. 27, 1970, p. 9.

De St. Jorre, John. "Biafra: the untold scandal," Observer (London), Jan. 16, 1972, p. 9.

_____ "Lagos has MIGS and Canberras, says flying Count," Observer (London), July 6, 1969, p. 2.
Count von Rosen was a Swedish pilot who fought for the Biafrans.

_____ "Looking for mercenaries (and some penportraits of those we found)," Transition (Kampala), VII, No. 33 (1967), 19-25.

Debré, François. "Biafra gets its second wind," Le Monde (Weekly edition - English), Dec. 10, 1969, pp. 1 & 8.
Improvement of the Biafran military situation despite the ravaging starvation.

_____ "Final phases of collapse," Le Monde (Weekly edition - English), Jan. 14, 1970, pp. 1 & 8.
The final events in the Biafran surrender.

Decraene, Philippe. "Six mois après la fin de la guerre du Biafra," Le Monde, July 29, 1970, p. 4.
Reviews the political and economic situation in the East Central State six months after the war.

Dent, Martin. "Nigeria after the war," World Today, XXVI (March 1970), 103-9.

Diallo, S. "Faut-il avoir peur du Nigéria?" Jeune Afrique, No. 509 (Oct. 6, 1970), 34-6.

"Diplomatic drums: inter-African contacts quicken in the wake of the Nigerian Civil War," Christian Sci. Mon., June 4, 1970, p. 4.

(MILITARY OPERATIONS AND THE AFTERMATH)

Dupuis, F. "Biafra: la résistance," Evénement (Paris), No. 32 (1968), 45-7.


Effiong, Noah M. "The Nigerian Civil War and the gullibles," Africa Today (March 1970), 5-7.


"Effiong speaks," Peace News (London), No. 1769 (May 22, 1970), 6-7.
    Major-General Effiong, second in command to the Biafran leader, announced the surrender of the secessionist state to the Federal troops on Jan. 12, 1970.


Egbuna, Obi. The Murder of Nigeria: an indictment. London: Panaf Publications, 1968. 31 p. (A Panaf pamphlet.)
    Virulent denunciation of the Nigerian military objectives and campaigns by an Ibo novelist and playwright.


Ejindu, Dennis D. "Report from inside," Africa and the World, (Aug. 1967), 3; 30-1.


Enahoro, Peter. "Lagos feels the strain," Spectator, (Jan. 24, 1969), 101-2.
    The author, former editor of the Nigerian leading newspaper, Daily Times, went into a voluntary exile in Europe rather than support the Federal use of force in quelling the rebellion.


"End of Biafra," National Review, XXII (Jan. 27, 1970), 72-3.


Enu, Cosmas E. "The Effects of the Nigerian Civil War on library services in the former Eastern Region," Libri, XX, No. 3 (1970), 206-17.
    The author is a Readers Services Librarian, University of Nigeria, Nsukka.


"Escalation urged," Globe & Mail, (Canada), Sept. 22, 1969, p. 2.
    Having renounced his support for Biafra, Dr. Azikiwe is reported to have urged the use of more sophisticated weapons by the Federal troops to hasten the end of the war.


Feuillet, C. "Afrique du Sud, Vietnam, Moyen-Orient, Biafra...d'où viennent les

(MILITARY OPERATIONS AND THE AFTERMATH)

armes?" <u>Jeune Afrique</u>, No. 441 (June 22, 1969), 60-5.

Feuser, W. "Requiem for Nigeria. A dossier on the role of the British and American press in the Nigerian war of reunification," <u>Afrique Nouvelle</u> (Paris), No. 32 (Oct. 1968), 35-48.

Forsyth, Frederick. "Report from the battle front," <u>Spectator</u>, CCXXIII (Dec. 20, 1969), 863-4.
An eye-witness account by the author of the <u>Biafra story</u> (1969).

Fuller, W. H. "Civil war aftermath; return to life," <u>Christianity Today</u>, XIV (June 5, 1970), 40.

"Goodbye to Biafra?" <u>Economist</u> (August 5, 1967), 471-2.

Hall, Richard. "Biafra's end: a personal narrative," <u>Sunday Times</u> (London), Jan. 18, 1970, p. 13.

Hanning, Hugh. "Lessons from the arms race," <u>Africa Report</u>, (Feb. 1968), 42-7.

_____ "Nigeria: a lesson from the arms race," <u>World Today</u>, XXIII (Nov. 1967), 465-72.

Hatch, John. "Nigeria's suicide," <u>New Statesman</u> (Aug. 18, 1967), 194-5.

_____ "Reuniting Nigeria," <u>New Statesman</u>, LXXIX (Jan. 23, 1970), 104-5.

Hoare, M. "No place for mercenaries," <u>Africa Report</u>, XIII (June 1968), 44-5.

Horgan, John. "Burying Biafra," <u>Commonweal</u>, XC (Feb. 20, 1970), 551-3.

(MILITARY OPERATIONS AND THE AFTERMATH)

"How secession collapsed," West Africa, No. 2746 (Jan. 17, 1970), 89-90.
    Recapitulates the final stages in the Biafran surrender.

Howe, Russell Warren. "Massacre in Nigeria," New Republic (Feb. 1968), 15-17.

"Ibo drums roll an end to secession," National Observer (U.S.), Jan. 19, 1970, p. 14.
    Reviews the causes and results of the war and its impact on Africa.

"Ibos come out of a trance," West Africa, No. 2749 (Feb. 7, 1970), 154-5.
    Life at Enugu following the end of the war.

Ikoku, S. G. "Nigeria tomorrow," West Africa, No. 2679 (Oct. 5, 1969), 1170-1.

Irele, Abiola. "The Nigerian Civil War and international opinion," Legon Observer,
    IV, No. 13 (1969), 2-6; No. 14 (1969), 11-14.

Jackson, E. "The Fall of Nsukka," Towards one Nigeria (Lagos), No. 3 (1967),
    13-14.
    A university town in the East Central State.

Johansson, Betram. "Thant defends visit; how much is known about Biafra's fate?"
    Christian Sci. Mon., Jan. 19, 1970, p. 3.
    Critical of the role of the United Nations and U Thant in the war.

Kemp, G. Arms traffic and third world conflicts. New York: Carnegie Endowment
    for International Peace, International Conciliation, 1970. 80 p. (No. 577.)

King, P. T. "Wanted: an African integrated force," African Review (Accra) I (May
    1965), 22-5; 90-4.

Kirk-Greene, A. H. M. "The War of a thousand days," Blackwood's Magazine,
    (March 1970), 193-207.

(MILITARY OPERATIONS AND THE AFTERMATH)

Kronenfeld, David B. "Different view on Biafra war," <u>L.A. Times</u>, Jan. 24, 1970, Part 2, p. 4.
Critical of the Federal war efforts and objectives, justifying the secession.

Kumulu, J. "Operational code of conduct for the Nigerian Armed Forces," <u>Towards one Nigeria</u> (Lagos), No. 3 (1967), 4-6.

Lake, Michael. "Biafra; the morals of investment," <u>Guardian</u> (Manchester) Jan. 15, 1970, p. 13.

Laptev, V. "Lessons of the Nigeria tragedy," <u>Int. Affairs</u> (Moscow), No. 4 (April 1969), 52 +.

"The Last days of Biafra," <u>Life,</u> LXVIII (Jan. 23, 1970), 20-7.
Includes many illustrations.

Leapman, Michael. "Biafra: at the front," <u>Venture</u> (July 1969), 11-13.

_____ "Nigerian Civil War in retrospect," <u>Venture</u>, XXII (April 1970), 17-22.

Legum, Colin. "Ibos start to pick up the pieces," <u>Observer</u> (London), Jan. 25, 1970, p. 1.
The Ibos have to start life afresh, having lost everything in the war.

_____ "Problems of reconstruction," <u>Current</u> (U.S.), CXVI (March 1970), 47-51.

Lerner, Max. "Biafra has been killed but heartbreak will remain," <u>L.A. Times,</u> Jan. 14, 1970, Part 2, p. 7.
The syndicated American newspaper columnist criticizes the world's indifference to Ibo sufferings, and recapitulates their goals in the war, eulogizing their courage, endurance and idealism.

(MILITARY OPERATIONS AND AFTERMATH)

Letiche, John M. <u>The Key problems of economic reconstruction and development in Nigeria; an address given under the auspices of the Nigerian Institute of International Affairs, Lagos, on 26 Sept., 1968.</u> Lagos: Nigerian Institute of International Affairs, 1968. 24 p.
Disputes the contention of leading Nigerian economists that inflation or deflation would constitute Nigeria's greatest post-war economic danger. Dr. Letiche is Professor of International Economics, University of California, Berkeley, and former Technical Adviser to the United Nations Economic Commission for Africa.

Lewis, Anthony. "How pointless it all seems now," <u>N.Y. Times Magazine</u> (Feb. 8, 1970), 26-7.
Personal experiences in the former secessionist state soon after the war.

Lewis, Roy. "Punishment for disloyal Nigerians," <u>Times</u> (London), Aug. 17, 1970, p. 1.
Active supporters of the secession.

Lindsay, Kennedy. "Guerilla warfare in Biafra," <u>Venture,</u> (Sept. 1969), 14-16.

_____ "How Biafra pays for the war," <u>Venture</u> (March 1969), 26-8.

Madaule, Jacques. "Encore le Biafra," <u>Le Monde</u>, Aug. 1, 1970, pp. 1 & 4.
Reviews the economic and political progress made in the East Central State since the end of the war.

Marienstras, R. "Biafra; la fin d'une nation," <u>Les Temps Modernes</u>, (Feb. 1970), 1169-73.

_____ "Une Génocide dans le sens de l'histoire," <u>Les Temps Modernes</u>, XXIV, No. 269 (1968), 769-77.

Martin, Kingsley. "Unsettled state," <u>New Statesman</u> (Aug. 9, 1968), 172-3.

(MILITARY OPERATIONS AND AFTERMATH)

Meisler, Stanley. "Biafra a year later - what didn't happen," <u>L.A. Times</u>, Jan. 17, 1971, Section A, pp. 1; 14-15.
The Federal leniency and magnanimity towards the former secessionists; fast rate of national reconciliation and Ibo economic resurgence.

_____ "Corruption in Nigeria has double edge," <u>L.A. Times</u>, Feb. 14, 1971, Section A, p. 16.
Widespread corruption and Nigerian Government's efforts to wipe it out.

_____ "Ibos struggle for slot in Nigerian society," <u>L.A. Times</u>, Feb. 21, 1971, Section I, p. 4.
Efforts of the Ibos to regain their jobs in the Federal Civil Service and the problems of reintegration.

_____ "The Nigeria which is not at war and the changes which will affect its future as much as the outcome of the war itself," <u>Africa Report</u>, XV (Jan. 1970), 16-17.
The impact of the war hardly felt in Lagos and Northern Nigeria.

_____ "Nigeria: war was only the 1st problem," <u>L.A. Times</u>, Feb. 8, 1970, Section G, p. 2.
Among the problems confronting Nigeria after the war are reintegration of the Ibos; military demobilization; creation of a new constitution acceptable to all states; curbing the increasing rate of murder, robbery, and unemployment.

_____ "Tribalism; cream rises to the top," <u>L.A. Times</u>, Aug. 2, 1970, Section G, p. 3.
Bribery and corruption in Nigeria.

Melloan, George. "I could see a bright future for the country," <u>National Observer</u> (U.S.), Jan. 19, 1970, pp. 1 & 14.
An excellent article optimistic of the future of Nigeria after reconstruction.

Miles, Jim. "Biafra: eye-witness report," <u>Catholic Review</u>, (Aug. 2, 1968), 1-2.

(MILITARY OPERATIONS AND AFTERMATH)

Morrison, Ian and Clive Callow. "Now time for the reconstruction," Times (London), Jan. 19, 1970, p. 23.
Appeals to all Nigerians to cooperate in rebuilding the country.

Murray, D. J. "Nigeria after Biafra," Current History, LVIII (March 1970), 135-44.

"New country on rise despite civil war," U.S. News & World Report, LXVI (June 16, 1969), 82-4.

Nigeria. Federal Ministry of Information. Second National Development Plan, 1970-74; programme of post-war reconstruction and development. Lagos: Govt. Printer, 1970. 344 p.

_____ No genocide: final report of observer team to Nigeria. Lagos, 1968.

_____ Operational code of conduct for Nigeria Armed Forces. Lagos, 1967. 5 p.
"Directive to all officers and men of the Armed Forces of the Federal Republic of Nigeria on conduct of military operations."
Despite the humane specifications of the code, it happened that in the heat of the battle, the code was occasionally ignored. Some offenders were punished.

Nigeria, Mid-Western. Ministry of Internal Affairs and Information. 100 days of liberated Mid-West. Benin City, 1968. 54 p.
The recapture of the state from the secessionist forces by the Federal troops.

"Le Nigeria a toujours des problèmes avec son ex-Biafra," Afrique Nouvelle (July 9-15, 1970), 7.

"Nigeria/Biafra armed conflict with a vengeance," Rev. Int. Comm. Jur., No. 2 (1969), 11-13.

"Nigeria-collapse of Biafra resistance in civil war - formal end of secession," Keesing's Cont. Arch., (March 14-21, 1970), 23869-71.
Chronological account of the final stages of Biafra's resistance.

# Nigerian Civil War: An Annotated Bibliography

(MILITARY OPERATIONS AND AFTERMATH)

"Nigeria - Enugu captured," _Afr. Res. Bull._, IV, No. 10 (1967), 887-9.

"Nigeria shaken by week of rioting," _Washington Post_, Sept. 22, 1969, p. A 14.
Rioting in Western Nigeria officially attributed to rioters' displeasure at their
increased taxes; but regarded by Western observers as symptomatic of Western
Nigerians' disgust with the endless civil war.

"Nigeria strives for brotherhood," _San Francisco Chronicle_, Feb. 16, 1970, p. 7.
National reconciliation.

"Nigeria war aftermath," _Facts on File_ (Jan. 22-28, 1970), 29-30; (Jan. 29-Feb. 4,
1970), 47.

"Nigeria: war orphans," _Africa_ (Africa Journal Ltd., London) (Oct. 1971), 36-8.
Plight of orphans in the Eastern States of Nigeria.

"Nigerian civil war ends," _Afr. Res. Bull._, VII (Feb. 15, 1970), 1642-52.
Chronology of final events.

"Nigeria's double D-Day," _West Africa_, No. 2652 (March 30, 1968), 361-2.
March 31, 1968, was the historic day in which the 12 state structure officially took
effect, superseding former four Regions.

"No Biafran genocide, U.N. reports," _National Catholic Reporter_, V (Jan. 29, 1969),
3.

Nwafor, B. U. "Recorded knowledge; a war casualty, an account of library devastation
during the Nigerian Civil War," _Library J._, XCVI (Jan. 1, 1971), 42-5.
Includes other historical examples of library destruction in war and photographs of
library victims in the Nigerian war. The author is a librarian at the University of
Nigeria, Nsukka.

Nzegwu, Henry. "Genocide or war? A Biafran accuses," _New African_, LI (1968),
8-9.

(MILITARY OPERATIONS AND AFTERMATH)

Obi, Dorothy S.   "Rebuilding with books in Nigeria," <u>Pennsylvania Library Associa-</u>
<u>tion Bulletin</u>, XXVI  (May 1971),  164-6.
Examines the problems of rebuilding libraries in former Biafra destroyed in the
war.  The author is a  doctoral student in Library Science, University of Pittsburgh, in the United States.

Oderinde, N. O.  "Nigerian libraries in post-war reconstruction," <u>Lagos Librarian,</u>
III  (Dec. 1968),  9-20.

Ofoegbu, Raymond R.  <u>Living together in Africa, Book one.</u>  New York: The Conch
Magazine, 1972.  (Conch African monograph series. )

_____  "Programme-oriented political system for Nigeria," <u>Nigerian Opinion,</u>  VI
(Aug./Oct. 1970),  74-83.

Okpa-Iroha, N.  "Reconstruction of devastated library services in war-affected areas
of Nigeria," <u>Library Association Record,</u>  LXXIII  (June 1971),  108-9.

Omu, F. I. A.  "The Nigerian press and the Great War," <u>Nigeria Magazine</u>,  No. 96
(1968),  44-9.

"1 dead, 180 arrested near Ibadan as Nigerian farmers protext taxes," <u>Globe & Mail</u>,
(Canada), Sept. 22, 1969, p. 2.
Foreign observers contend that the protest had a deep-seated reason - popular dis-
satisfaction with the war.

Onyia, E. I.  "Un Drama ignoroto: la guerra Nigeria-Biafra," <u>Il Mulino,</u>  (April 1968),
293-310.

"Operation Biafra baby," <u>Newsweek</u>,  LXXIII (June 9, 1969),  60.
The operation of small mini-con planes that constituted the Biafran Air Force in
June 1969, was named after the starving Biafran children.

(MILITARY OPERATIONS AND AFTERMATH)

Osinibi, O. "Nigeria's new Army," West Africa, No. 2755 (March 28, 1970), 336.
The problem of demobilisation.

"La Parole est aux armes," Afrique Express (Bruxelles), IX (May 10, 1969), 9-11.

Person, Y. "Génocide et unité nationale: la tragédie du Biafra," Les Temps Modernes (Dec. 1968), 1055-71.

Rake, Alan. "Nigeria after the war," African Development (London), (Feb. 1970), 9-15.

Renard, A. "Le Nigéria à l'heure du défi biafrais," Projet, Civilisation, Travail, Economie (Paris), No. 25 (1968), 598-606.

"Return of the Ibos," West Africa, No. 2747 (Jan. 24, 1970), 93.
Their reintegration into the Nigerian society after the war.
See also West Africa (Jan. 24, 1970), 94-5, for the situation in former Biafra just after the war.

Sanders, Charles L. "The War between blacks that nobody cares about," Jet (Chicago), (July 27, 1967), 14-18.

Schwarz, Walter. "Ojukwu the moderate," Manchester Guardian, Jan. 17, 1970, p. 4.
Reviews the political impact of the Biafran defeat; the objectives of the secessionists; the personality of their leader; and pays tribute to their courage and endurance.

"Seven reasons why I quit the rebel camp - U.S. agent Goldstein," Daily Times (Lagos), Aug. 17, 1968, p. 2.
An American soldier of fortune outlines the reasons for his ceasing to fight for the Biafrans.

Shepherd, G. W. "Civil wars and the international arms traffic," Africa Today, XIV, No. 6 (1967), 5.

Signaté, I. "Fédéraux et Biafrais reapprennent à y vivre," Jeune Afrique (Paris),

(MILITARY OPERATIONS AND AFTERMATH)

No. 475 (Feb. 10, 1970), 25-6.

"Softening the blow of Biafra's defeat," Observer (London), Jan. 18, 1970, p. 4.

Stokke, Olav. "System transformation in Nigeria," Coop. & Conflict, VI, Nos. 3-4 (1971), 147-71.
Processes of integration and disintegration within the Federation up to the secession.

"La Tension entre la capitale et l'état de l'Ouest menace l'unité nationale," Le Monde (Weekly edition - French), Nov. 19-25, 1970, p. 3.
Some prominent Yorubas and supporters of Chief Obafemi Awolowo reported unhappy about the decision of the Federal Government to hand over power to the civilian government in 1976 and not to create more states from the Western State.

Thompson, W. F. K. "Nigeria's way to nationhood," Daily Telegraph (Britain), Jan. 17, 1970, p. 12.
Bright future for Nigeria despite the war.

U.S. Dept. of the Army. Area handbook for Nigeria, prepared by Foreign Area Studies, American University. Washington, D.C., 1972. 485 p.
"This volume is one of a series of handbooks prepared by Foreign Area Studies (FAS) of the American University, designed to be useful to military and other personnel who need a convenient compilation of basic facts about social, economic, political, and military institutions and practices of various countries. The emphasis is on objective description of nation's present society and the kinds of possible or probable changes that might be expected in the future." (Foreword)
Supersedes the March 1964 edition. Includes a very extensive bibliography classified by subject, a glossary of terms and index.

Uphoff, N. T. and H. Ottenmoeller. "After the Nigerian Civil War; with malice towards whom," Africa Today, (March 1970), 1-40.

Uwechue, Raph. "Une Guerre africaine," Jeune Afrique, No. 442 (June 29, 1969), 22.

(MILITARY OPERATIONS AND AFTERMATH)

Uwechue, Raph. "Les Uns profitent de la guerre, les autres ne veulent pas la paix," Jeune Afrique, No. 401 (Sept. 15, 1968), 20-3.

Van der Post, Laurens. The Prisoner and the bomb. New York: Morrow, 1971. 152 p.

"Waffenschmuggel," Der Spiegel (Hamburg), No. 48 (Nov. 21, 1966), 136-8.

"We died like flies in Biafra jail," Observer (London), Jan. 18, 1970, p. 1. Impressions of prisoners released from jail at the end of the war.

Wells, Alan. Nation building models and the Nigerian dilemma. New Orleans: Dept. of Sociology, Tulane University, 1971. 33 p. Paper presented at the Annual Meeting of the American Sociological Association, Denver, 1971.

Whiteman, Kaye. "Nigeria's war; history takes over," Venture, XXIV (Jan. 1972), 26-9. Reviews recent publications on the war, noting the paucity of first hand information.

"Who rules Biafra now?" New Statesman (Jan. 16, 1970), 1-2.

"Will Nigeria collapse?" Illus. Lond. News, CCLVI (Jan. 31, 1970), 9. Current military and political situation; post-war problems; Nigerian economic strength hardly affected by the war.

Wolf, Jean and C. Brovelli. La Guerre des rapaces. La vérité sur la guerre du Biafra. Paris: Michel, 1969. 288 p.

Wolfers, Michael. "Nigeria's legacy of war," Times (London), Nov. 19, 1971, p. 14.

"The Word and the war," West Africa, No. 2698 (Feb. 15, 1969), 169-70.

(MILITARY OPERATIONS AND AFTERMATH)


Yannopoulos, T. "Luttes de classes et guerre nationale au Nigéria," Rev. Fr. Sci. Pol., XVIII (June 1968), 508-23.


"Zik on military rule," West Africa, No. 2991 (Nov. 6, 1972), 1505.
At the First Samuel Jereton Mariere Memorial Lecture entitled "Stability in Nigeria after the military rule - an analysis of political theory," Dr. Azikiwe suggested the establishment of a civilian-military government after 1976 for an experimental period of five years at the end of which a referendum should be conducted to determine whether the joint rule should continue or be abrogated. The Nigerian scholars opposed to this view contend that this will be tantamount to perpetuation of the military regime which is only designed to serve as an interregnum before the establishment of a civilian government and whose most important asset is their possession of force rather than their administrative capability.

# Nigerian Civil War: An Annotated Bibliography

SOME KEY PERSONALITIES DIRECTLY OF INDIRECTLY CONNECTED WITH THE
WAR

Aguiyi-Ironsi, Johnson T., an Ibo (1924-1966).
First Nigerian to hold the rank of Major-General and Supreme Commander of the
Armed Forces. Commander of all U.N. Peace Keeping Force in the Congo, now
Zaire, 1960-61. Head of the Federal Military Government, Jan. 16-July 29, 1966,
when he was assassinated in the country's second military coup. A tough, bluff,
British-trained professional who firmly believed that military men are not trained
for politics and should leave it to politicians. Strongly convinced that strong
regionalism was the bane of the First Nigerian Republic, he sought to submerge
regional loyalty by moving towards a more unitary form of administration. Thus on
May 24, 1966, he promulgated the controversial decree which reads in part:
> The former regions are abolished, and Nigeria grouped into a number of territori-
> al areas called "provinces." Nigeria ceases to be what has been described as a
> Federation. It now becomes simply the Republic of Nigeria... Every civil
> servant is now called upon to see his function in any part of Nigeria in which he
> is serving in the context of the whole country.
The opposition to this decree by Northern Nigeria was the most important factor in
the rioting against the Eastern Nigerians living in the region.

Akintola, Samuel, a Yoruba (1910-1966).
A shrewd politician whose mismanagement of the Western Nigerian elections during
his incumbency as Premier of the Region called in the military to quell the crisis
in the area and topple the national civilian government, thus paving the way for the
Civil War. Founding member of the Action Group Party in 1950, Deputy leader of
the Party from 1954 till he broke with Chief Awolowo, leader of the Party, to found
the Nigerian National Democratic Party closely allied with the Northern People's
Congress. Federal Minister of Labor, 1951-52; Federal Minister of Health, 1953;
Leader of the Opposition in the Federal House of Representatives, 1954-57; Federal
Minister of Communications and Aviation, 1957-59; Premier of Western Nigeria,
1959-Jan. 15, 1966, when he was assassinated in the first military coup.

Arikpo, Okoi, an Ekoi (1916- ).
A brilliant Ph.D. in Anthropology, currently Nigerian Commissioner for External
Affairs, he took an active part in peace negotiations with Biafra; specially note-
worthy is his 13 page speech, entitled <u>A Testimony of Faith,</u> delivered before the
General Assembly of the United Nations on October 11, 1968, in which he recounts
various peace efforts made by the Federal Government to end the war and restates
the official Nigerian position in the war - reunification of the country based upon
Biafra's renunciation of its secession.

(SOME KEY PERSONALITIES...)

Studied at Government College, Unuahia; Yaba Higher College; University of London.
Elected to the Eastern House of Assembly in 1951 as an independent, "adopted" by
the N. C. N. C. and sent to the House of Representatives; Nigeria's first Minister of
Lands, Survey and Local Development and later Minister of Mines.  First Secretary
of National Universities Commission.  Author of The Development of Modern
Nigeria (1967).

Asika, Ukpabi, an Ibo (1936- ).
Administrator of the East Central State, he remained loyal to the Federal Govern-
ment throughout the war.  Studied Economics at the University of Ibadan and
Political Science at the University of California, Los Angeles.  Lecturer at the
University of Ibadan till 1967 when he was appointed Administrator of his  State.
His 80 page book No Victors; No Vanquished: Opinions (1968) comprises chiefly
his interviews and speeches.  His reasons for supporting the Federal Government
are clearly indicated in his article, "Why I am a Federalist," Transition, VII,
No. 36 (1968), 39-44; Insight (Lagos), (Oct. 1968), 7-14.  His other work is a
booklet entitled Reflections on the Political Evolution of One Nigeria (1969).

Awolowo, Obafemi, a Yoruba (1909- ).
One of the pioneers of Nigerian independence and founder of the Action Group
Party in 1950.  Nigeria's Finance Commissioner and Vice-Chairman of the Federal
Executive Council during the war, taking one of the strongest stands against the
secession.  His historical justification of starvation as a weapon of warfare was
very controversial.  Studied for a degree in commerce as a private student and
Law in London, being called to the Bar in 1947.  President of his Party, Action
Group, and its leader in Western House of Assembly, 1952-54; Premier and Minister
of Finance for Western Region, 1954-59; Leader of Opposition in the Federal
Parliament, 1959-Nov. 1962, when he and 28 other members of his Party were put
on trial on charge of treasonable felony.  Convicted and sentenced to ten years
imprisonment, Sept. 1963, but granted a State pardon and released from prison in
August 1966.  Head of Western Nigeria's delegation to All Nigeria Ad Hoc Constitutional Conference in Lagos, Sept. 1966.
Author of numerous works, most important of which are his Path to Nigerian Freedom (1947); Awo; the Autobiography (1960); Thoughts on the Nigerian Constitution
(1966); The People's Republic (1968); The Strategy and Tactics of People's Republic
of Nigeria (1970).

Azikiwe, Nnamdi, an Ibo (1904- ).
Former Governor-General of Nigeria, 1960-1963, and President of the Republic
when it was overthrown in the military coup of Jan. 15, 1966, although he was out

(SOME KEY PERSONALITIES...)

of the country for medical treatment. On Nov. 9, 1967, he announced his support of Biafra's claim to right of self-determination. On Feb. 1969, at Rhodes House, Oxford, he called for an international action to end the war, suggesting also the use of plebiscite to determine the loyalty of the minority people in the secessionist state. The peace plan was rejected by the Nigerian Government on the ground that it would constitute an interference in the internal affairs of the country. In August, 1969, he renounced his support of Biafra and urged his fellow Ibos to give up their bid for independence and seek accommodation with the Federal Government. This switch was a serious diplomatic blow to the secessionists.
Educated at Howard, Lincoln, Pennsylvania and Columbia Universities, 1925-32; Founder and editor, African Morning Post, Accra, 1934-37; Founder and editor, West African Pilot, Lagos, 1937-47; Secretary-General, N.C.N.C., 1944-46; National President, N.C.N.C., 1946-1960. Leader of the N.C.N.C. delegations to the Colonial Office, London, for review of Nigerian constitution, 1947, 1953, 1954, 1957, 1958 and 1960. Author of numerous books, articles and scholarly papers; his major works include Liberia in world politics (1932); Renascent Africa (1937); Zik: a selection from the speeches of Dr. Nnamdi Azikiwe (1961); My Odyssey: an autobiography (1971); Military revolution in Nigeria (1973). Former Chancellor of the University of Nigeria; currently Chancellor of Lagos University.


Balewa, Abubakar Tafawa, an Hausa (1912-1966).
The first Prime Minister of Nigeria, 1957-1966, killed in the Jan. 1966 military coup. By temperament a moderate; the leaders of the coup blamed him for not intervening in the political crisis in Western Nigeria during the 1965 West Regional elections. Deeply religious, quiet and contemplative, he was drawn into politics in 1946 when he was elected to Northern House of Assembly. Studied at Katsina Training College, 1928; Teacher and Headmaster, Bauchi Middle School, 1933-45; Institute of Education, London University, 1945; Member of the Federal Legislative Council, 1947; Federal Minister of Works, 1952-53; Deputy Leader of the Northern People's Congress. Author of a novel, Shaihu Umar (1934), written in Hausa but translated into English by Mervyn Hiskett and published in 1967 by Longmans - a critical portrayal of Hausa life and Islamic society. Another work is a collection of speeches, Nigeria speaks; speeches made between 1957 and 1964, (1964). Chancellor of the University of Ibadan, 1962-1966.


Bello, Ahmadu, Sardauna of Sokoto, a Fulani (1909-1966).
Premier of Northern Nigeria, 1954-1966; born of an aristocratic family and a descendant of the great Fulani scholar, Usman Dan Fodio, founder of the Fulani Empire; proud, often uncompromising. Educated at Katsina Training College, 1926-31; teacher, Sokoto Middle School, 1931-34; appointed Sarduana of Sokoto and member of Sokoto Native Administration Council, 1938; elected to the Northern

(SOME KEY PERSONALITIES...)

House of Assembly, 1949; founder and President of Northern People's Congress, 1949-1966; elected to Federal House of Representatives, 1952-54. He was assassinated on Jan. 15, 1966, in the military coup, having exerted an enormous influence on Nigerian politics; his political Party was closely allied with Akintola's Nigerian National Democratic Party that plunged Western Nigeria into a political chaos during the Regional elections of 1965. His only known work is his autobiography, My life (1962). See also Stanley Diamond's "The Sardauna of Sokoto," Africa Today, X, (April 1963), 12-14.

Dike, Kenneth Onwuka, an Ibo historian (1917- ).
Never a politician though he served as Roving Ambassador for Biafra. Educated at Achimota College (Ghana); Fourabay College, Sierra Leone; University of Durham and University of London where he obtained his Ph.D. in History in 1950. Lecturer, University of Ibadan, 1950-52; Senior Lecturer, 1954-56, and Professor, University of Ibadan, 1956-60; Principal of the university, 1958-60; Vice-Chancellor, 1960-66. Senior Research Fellow, West African Institute of Social and Economic Research, 1952-54; Founder and Director of Nigerian National Archives, 1951-64; Chairman of Nigerian Antiquities Commission, 1954-66; President of the Historical Society of Nigeria, 1955-69; Director of the Institute of African Studies, University of Ibadan, 1960-67; Fellow of Royal Historical Society and currently Professor of African History, Harvard University, in U.S.A.
Author of Report on the preservation and administration of historical records and establishment of a Public Records Office in Nigeria (1954); Trade and politics in the Niger Delta, 1830-1885 (1956); Origins of the Niger Mission (1957); A Hundred years of British rule in Nigeria (1960.

Elias, Taslim Olawale, a Yoruba (1914- ).
Former Attorney-General of Nigeria and former Professor and Dean of the Faculty of Law, University of Lagos, and currently the Chief Justice of Nigeria, he is considered the most distinguished African legal scholar. As Federal Attorney-General during the war he was solely concerned with legal and constitutional aspects of the war. Studied at the University of London, and called to the Bar, 1947; Senior Research Fellow, University of Manchester, 1951-53; Oppenheim Research Fellow, Oxford University, 1954-60; Visiting Professor of Political Science, University of Delhi, 1956; Member of the Nigerian delegation to the constitutional conference in London, 1958; Federal Attorney-General, 1960-72; Chief Justice, 1972-. The first West African to gain a Ph.D. degree in Law from the University of London and the first African to be awarded the LLD degree of London University by submission of publications. An internationally known constitutional and international lawyer, he served as Chairman of U.N. Committee of Constitutional Experts to Draft Congo Constitution, 1961-62, and as Chairman of the Committee of U.N. Conference on Law of Treaties, 1968-69. He is President of Nigerian Society of

(SOME KEY PERSONALITIES...)

international law.
Some of his many publications include <u>Nigerian land law and custom</u> (1951, 3rd ed.,
1962); <u>Groundwork of Nigerian law</u> (1954, revised and published as <u>Nigerian legal</u>
<u>system</u>, 1963); <u>The nature of African customary law</u> (1956); <u>The impact of English</u>
<u>law on Nigerian customary law and customs</u> (1960); <u>British colonial law; a compara-</u>
<u>tive study of the interaction between English and local laws in British Dependencies</u>
(1962); <u>Ghana and Sierra Leone: the development of their laws and constitutions</u>
(1962); <u>Nigeria: development of its laws and constitution</u> (1967). Editor, <u>Nigerian</u>
<u>press law</u> (1969); <u>The prison systems in Nigeria; papers submitted at the National</u>
<u>Conference on Prison System, July 1-5, 1968</u> (1969); Editor, <u>Law and Social Change</u>
<u>in Nigeria</u> (1972).

Enahoro, Anthony, an Edo (1923- ).
Former Deputy leader of the Action Group Party and currently Nigerian Commissioner for Information and Labour. An articulate, persuasive speaker, he was the
Federal Chief delegate to peace talks with Biafra. He contended that no peace efforts could be meaningful until the Biafrans renounced their independence and accepted the principle of a united Nigeria, as outlined in <u>Framework for settlement:</u>
<u>the Federal case in Kampala</u> (1968).
Editor, <u>Southern Nigeria defender</u>, 1944-45; editor, <u>the Daily comet</u>, 1945-47;
editor, <u>the West African Pilot</u>, 1946; editor, <u>Nigerian star</u>, 1950-53; first Ishan
member of the Western House of Assembly, 1951; member of the Federal House of
Representatives, 1951-54; Minister of Home Affairs, Western Nigeria, 1954; Chairman of the Mid-West Advisory Council established to represent minority interests
of the area, 1958; Member of Parliament, 1959; sentenced to seven years' imprisonment along with some 28 members of the Action Group Party for allegedly plotting
to overthrow the Federal Government, 1963; granted a State pardon and released
from prison, August 1966; leader of the Mid-West delegation to All-Nigeria Ad Hoc
Constitutional Conference, Sept. 1966.
Author of <u>Nnamdi Azikiwe, saint or sinner?</u> (1948); <u>Fugitive offender; the story of a</u>
<u>political prisoner</u> (1965) written in prison, reviewing the circumstances of his ar-
rest, trial and conviction on a treasobale felony charge, the pros and cons of a
single party system and factors that hinder the attainment of African unity.

Gowon, Yakubu, Angas (1934- ).
General, Supreme Commander of the Armed Forces and Head of the Federal
Military Government. Of a strong religious up-bringing and generally regarded as
a moderate, he unwaveringly held to the belief throughout the war that it was his
duty to keep Nigeria one and united, thus preserving national territorial boundaries
and preventing the break-up of the country. He declared, "As far as I am concerned,
I am fighting a war to keep the country one and united. I therefore cannot afford to
be callous in the way I prosecute the war." (Time XCIV [July 4, 1964], 32).

(SOME KEY PERSONALITIES...)

This is borne out by his magnanimity in victory.
Attended Zaria Government Secondary School; joined the Nigerian Army, 1954;
trained at Eaton Hall, Cheshire, England, 1955; Member of the Nigerian contigent
in the Congo (now Zaire) as part of U.N. Peace Keeping Force, 1960; military
course at Staff College, Camberley, Surrey, 1962; Lt. Colonel, 1963; Chief of Staff,
Army Headquarters, 1966; Head of the Federal Military Government, August 1,
1966-. For his further views on the crisis, see his Let us reconcile; broadcast on
January 1970, following formal surrender by the rebels (1970), and Gowon's Spotlight on the future of the Ibos (1967).

Mbanefo, Louis Nwachukwu, an Ibo (May 1911- ).
The first indigenous Chief Justice of Eastern Nigeria, 1959; former International
Court Judge, he served as Biafra's Chief delegate to the peace talks with Federal
Nigeria on some occasions. He comes from an aristocratic family in Onitsha.
Studied at London and Cambridge Universities and called to the Bar, 1935; the first
Ibo lawyer; Member of the old Nigerian Legislative Council, 1949-51; Judge of
Nigerian Supreme Court, 1952.

Njoku, Eni, an Ibo (1917- ).
Holder of a doctorate in Botany and one of Nigeria's best known scientists; served
as Biafra's Chief peace delegate during most of the peace talks with Federal
Nigeria; former Vice-Chancellor of the Universities of Lagos and Nigeria, Nsukka;
studied Hope Waddell College, Calabar; Yaba Higher College; University of Manchester, 1944-48; Lecturer, University of Ibadan, 1948-52; Minister of Mines and
Power, 1952-53; Senior Lecturer and Professor of Botany, University of Ibadan,
1953-62; Chairman of Electricity Corporation of Nigeria, 1956-62; President of
Science Association of Nigeria, 1959-60; Member of Superior Academic Council of
the University of Lovanium, Kinshasa, 1963-66; leader of Eastern Nigerian delegation to All-Nigeria Ad Hoc Constitutional Conference in Lagos, September 1966,
former Professor of Botany, University of Nigeria, Nsukka. Author of Plant
life in tropical environment (1954).

Ojukwu, Odumegwu, an Ibo (1933- ).
General of the Biafran Army and leader of Biafra, he was the most controversial
figure during the war. To his opponents, he was a wealthy (son of a millionaire),
arrogant, ambitious young man bent upon the destruction of the Nigerian Federation
for his political ambitions; to his supporters, he was their savior, a "Deus ex
Machina," who claimed that the war was not simply a conflict over the constitutional
guarantee of the territorial integrity of his state, but the survival of the Ibos themselves. He contended that his foreign critics had deliberately ignored the basic
goals of his state which were "not simply to win independence but to establish a new,
more African-type society and to secure a more equitable political system based

upon sounder economic relations between African states and Europe." (Ahiara Declaration, 1969.)

Born at Zungeru, Northern Nigeria, though his home town is Nnewi, in the East Central State; attended King's College, Lagos; Epsom College, Surrey, England; Lincoln College, Oxford, where he obtained his master's degree in Modern History. Administrative Officer in Eastern Nigeria; joined the Nigerian Army, 1957, the first Nigerian university graduate to do so; Lieutenant, 1958; Instructor, African Frontier Force Training School at Teshie, Ghana; Major, 1961; Staff Officer in Nigerian First Brigade under the U.N. Peace Keeping Programme in the Congo (Zaire), 1962; Lieutenant-Colonel and Quartermaster-General, 1963; Military Governor of Eastern Nigeria, Jan. 17, 1966; attended the Aburi meeting with other Nigerian military leaders in Ghana, Jan. 4-5, 1967; proclaimed Biafran independence, May 30, 1967; promoted to the rank of General, June 1969; sought a political asylum in the Ivory Coast, one of the four African countries to recognize Biafra, Jan. 10, 1970.

Author of The Ahiara Declaration; the principles of the Biafran revolution (1969); Biafra; selected speeches and random thoughts of C. Odumegwu Ojukwu, with diaries of events, (1969). Both publications are the most important works on the war from the Biafran viewpoint.

Okotie-Eboh, Festus, Itsekiri-Urhobo (1912-1966).

One of the wealthiest Nigerians and Federal Minister of Finance, 1957-66; assassinated in the Jan. coup of 1966; studied business administration and chiropody (Czechoslavakia), 1948; established a shoe industry and a chain of secondary schools in Mid-Western Nigeria; Member of the Western House of Assembly, 1951-54; Chief Whip, N.C.N.C., in Western Legislature; leader, N.C.N.C. delegation to London Constitutional Conference, 1953; national treasurer, N.C.N.C., 1954; elected to Federal House of Representatives, 1954; Federal Minister of Labor and Welfare, 1955-57.

Okpara, Michael, an Ibo (1920- ).

Premier of Eastern Nigeria when the Nigerian civilian government was toppled in the military coup, Jan. 1966; Political Adviser to the Head of the Biafran Government; proud, fearless, and sometimes uncompromising.

Attended Uzuakoli Methodist College and studied medicine at Yaba Higher College; Government medical officer, 1948; private medical practitioner in Umuahia, 1949-53; elected to the Eastern House of Assembly on N.C.N.C. ticket, 1952; Minister of Health for Eastern Nigeria, 1954-59; Premier and leader of the N.C.N.C., 1959-66. A very powerful, articulate speaker, he was often impatient with conservative elements of the Northern People's Congress with which his Party was in alliance.

(SOME KEY PERSONALITIES...)

He was a strong advocate of what he termed "pragmatic socialism" - a belief that the salvation of Nigeria lies in agricultural revolution. Left the country on Jan. 10, 1970, on the fall of Biafra.

*Nigerian Civil War: An Annotated Bibliography*

APPENDIX I:  POPULATION STATISTICS


Population Statistics


1. The census results in Nigeria and its Regions (millions)

| Region | 1952-1953 | 1962 (unofficial) | 1963 | Area (in square miles) |
|---|---|---|---|---|
| Northern | 16.8 | 22.0 | 29.8 | 281,782 |
| Eastern | 7.2 | 12.3 | 12.4 | 29,484 |
| Western | 4.6 | 8.1 | 10.3 | 30,454 |
| Mid-Western | 1.5 | 2.4 | 2.4 | 14,922 |
| Lagos | 0.2 | 0.5 | 0.7 | 27 |
| Total | 30.3 | 45.3 | 55.7 | 356,669 |


2. The main tribes of Nigeria according to the 1952-1953 and 1963 censuses (thousands)

| Tribe | 1952-1953 | 1963 |
|---|---|---|
| Hausa | 5,544 | 11,653 |
| Ibo | 5,458 | 9,246 |
| Yoruba | 5,045 | 11,321 |
| Fulani | 3,030 | 4,784 |
| Kanuri | 1,301 | 2,259 |
| Tiv | 788 | 1,394 |
| Ibibio | 762 | 2,006 |
| Edo | 466 | 955 |
| Anang | 435 | 675 |
| Ijaw | 343 | 1,089 |

(APPENDIX I: POPULATION STATISTICS)

3A. Population of individual States based on the 1963 census.

| State | Capital | Area (in sq. miles) | Population | Density per sq. mile |
|-------|---------|---------------------|------------|----------------------|
| Western | Ibadan | 29,100 | 9,487,525 | 326 |
| North-Eastern | Bauchi | 103,639 | 7,793,443 | 75 |
| Central-Eastern | Enugu | 11,310 | 7,227,559 | 639 |
| Kano | Kano | 16,630 | 5,774,842 | 347 |
| North-Western | Sokoto | 65,143 | 5,733,296 | 88 |
| South-Eastern | Calabar | 11,166 | 3,622,589 | 324 |
| North-Central | Zaria | 27,08 | 4,098,305 | 151 |
| Benue-Plateau | Jos. | 40,590 | 4,009,408 | 99 |
| Mid-Western | Benin | 14,922 | 2,535,839 | 170 |
| Central-West | Ilorin | 28,672 | 2,399,365 | 84 |
| Rivers | Port Harcourt | 7,008 | 1,544,314 | 220 |
| Lagos | Lagos | 1,381 | 1,443,567 | 1,045 |
| TOTAL | | 356,669 | 55,670,052 | 156 |

3B. *Year of Census

| Year of Census | Total Population | Density per Sq. Mile |
|----------------|------------------|----------------------|
| 1911 | 15,966,000 | 42 |
| 1921 | 17,500,000 | 48 |
| 1931 | 19,930,000 | 54 |
| 1941 | 21,000,000 | 57 |
| 1951 | 25,000,000 | 67 |
| 1953 | 32,572,000 | 85 |
| 1958 | 34,700,000 | 98 |
| 1962/63 | 55,770,056 | 156 |
| 1969 | 68,000,000 (Estimated) | |

* Source: Nigerian Opinion (April 1973), p. 13.

# Nigerian Civil War: An Annotated Bibliography

4A.  [1]Cabinet Membership: Distribution by Ethnic Unit.

| *Ethnicity | Independence Cabinet | Immediate Pre-Coup Cabinet |
|---|---|---|
| 1. Hausa-Fulani (29%) | 39% | 31% |
| 2. Yoruba (20%) | 26% | 34% |
| 3. Ibo (17%) | 17% | 19% |
| 4. Tiv/Plateau (9%) | 4.3% | 3.1% |
| 5. Ibibio (6%) | 4.3% | 0 |
| 6. Kanuri (5%) | 4.3% | 9.8% |
| 7. Others (14%) | 23% | 32% |

*Ethnic units arranged in rank order of size within country, with the units' per-
cent of national population in parentheses.

1 Source: Donald G. Morrison, et al.  Black Africa: a comparative handbook (New York:
The Free Press, 1972), p. 315.

4B.  *Education 1966.

| Types of Institutions | Number of Institutions | Number of Teachers | Number of Students |
|---|---|---|---|
| Primary Schools | 14,907 | 91,049 | 3,025,981 |
| Secondary Schools | 1,350 | 11,644 | 211,305 |
| Technical Schools | 73 | 789 | 15,059 |
| Teacher Training Colleges | 193 | 1,837 | 30,493 |
| Universities (1971) | 6 | 2,628 | 17,495 |

* Source: Africa South of the Sahara 1973 (London: Europa Publications, 1973), p. 629.

APPENDIX II: EXCERPTS OF THE CONTROVERSIAL DECREE OF MAY 24, 1966

Excerpts of the Controversial decree of May 24, 1966, promulgated over a national radio broadcast by Major-General J. T. U. Aguiyi-Ironsi, the Supreme Commander of the Armed Forces and Head of the Federal Military Government.

It is now three months since the Government of the Federal Republic of Nigeria was handed over to the Armed Forces. Now that peace has been restored in the troubled areas it is time that the Military Government indicates clearly what it proposes to accomplish before relinquishing power. The removal of one of the obstacles on the way is provided for in the Constitution (Suspension and Modification) Decree (No. 5) 1966 which comes into effect at once. The provisions of the Decree are intended to remove the last vestiges of the intense regionalism of the recent past, and to produce that cohesion in the governmental structure which is so necessary in achieving and maintaining the paramount objective of the National Military Government, and indeed of every true Nigerian, namely, national unity.

The highlights of this Decree are as follows: the former regions are abolished, and Nigeria grouped into a number of territorial areas called provinces. Nigeria ceases to be what has been described as a federation. It now becomes simply the Republic of Nigeria. The former Federal Military Government and the Central Government and the Central Executive Council become respectively the National Military Government and the Executive Council. All the Military Governors are members of the Executive Council.

A Military Governor is assigned to a group of provinces over which, and subject to the direction and control of the Head of the National Military Government, he shall exercise executive power. In order to avoid any major dislocation of the present administration machinery, the grouping of the provinces is without prejudice to the Constitutional and Administrative arrangements to be embodied in the New Constitution in accordance with the wishes of the people of Nigeria.

The National Military Government assumes the exercise of all legislative powers throughout the Republic subject to such delegations to Military Governors as are considered necessary for purposes of efficient administration. The public services of the former federation and regions become unified into one national public service under a National Public Service Commission. There is a Provincial Service Commission for each group of provinces to which is delegated functions in respect of public officers below a given rank. This rather drastic change will probably involve a reconstitution of the existing commissions, and the National Military Government reserves the right to do so in the manner stipulated in the Decree... Every Civil Servant is now called upon to see his function in any part of Nigeria in which he is serving in the context of the whole country. The orientation should now be towards national unity and progress...

(APPENDIX II: EXCERPTS OF THE CONTROVERSIAL DECREE OF MAY 24, 1966)

As a corrective regime we must ensure that the fatal maladies of the past are cured before we relinquish power.  We propose as a last act to give the country an accurate count as well as a Constitution which will guarantee unity, freedom, and true democracy to all Nigerians everywhere.  Investigations are proceeding in respect of ex-politicians of the former regime.  Any of them found guilty will be dealt with according to law irrespective of their position in the community.  My Government will then consider utilizing the services of those who have not been found wanting and who are prepared to serve in the context of national unity.

APPENDIX III: TEXT OF BROADCAST BY MAJOR-GENERAL YAKUBU GOWON

Broadcast by Major-General Yakubu Gowon to the Nation on the Declaration of National Emergency and Creation of 12 States, on the 27th May, 1967.

Dear Countrymen:

As you are all aware, Nigeria has been immersed in an extremely grave crisis for almost eighteen months. We have now reached a most critical phase where what is at stake is the very survival of Nigeria as one political and economic unit. We must rise to the challenge and what we do in the next few days will be decisive.

The whole world is witness to the continued defiance of Federal Authority by the Government of Eastern Region, the disruption of the Railway, the Coal Corporation, the normal operations of the Nigerian Ports Authority, the interference with the flight schedules of the Nigeria Airways and other illegal acts by the Eastern Region Government culminating in the edicts promulgated last month by that Government purporting to seize all Federal Statutory Corporations and Federal revenues collected in the East.

The consequence of these illegal acts has been the increasing deterioration of the Nigerian economy. It has also produced uncertainty and insecurity generally and pushed the country with increasing tempo towards total disintegration and possible civil war and bloodshed on massive scale.

It has also led to increasing loss of foreign confidence in the ability of Nigerians to resolve the present problems. This has been reflected in the stoppage of the inflow of much badly needed additional foreign investment; it has put a brake on economic development so essential to the well-being of the common man and the ordinary citizen whose only desire is for peace and stability to carry on his daily work.

In the face of all these, I have shown great restraint hoping that through peaceful negotiations a solution acceptable to all sections of the country can be found. Unfortunately, the hopes of myself and my other colleagues on the Supreme Military Council have been disappointed by the ever increasing campaign of hate by the Governor of the Eastern Region. Lt.-Col. Ojukwu has continuously increased his demands as soon as some are met in order to perpetuate the crisis and lead the Eastern Region out of Nigeria. We know very well the tragic consequences of such a misguided step. Not only will the regions themselves disintegrate further, but before then pushed by foreign powers and mercenaries who will interfere; this dear country will be turned into a bloody stage for chaotic and wasteful civil war.

When the tragic events of 15th January, 1966, occurred, the country acquiesced in the installation of a Military Regime only because it desired that order and discipline

(APPENDIX III: TEXT OF BROADCAST BY MAJOR–GENERAL YAKUBU GOWON)

should be restored in the conduct of the affairs of this country, that swift reforms will be introduced to produce just and honest Government, to usher in stability and ensure fair treatment of all citizens in every part of the country. The citizens of this country have not given the Military Regime any mandate to divide up the country into sovereign states and to plunge them into bloody disaster.

As I have warned before, my duty is clear - faced with this final choice between action to save Nigeria and acquiescence in secession and disintegration. I am therefore proclaiming a State of Emergency throughout Nigeria with immediate effect. I have assumed full powers as Commander-in-Chief of the Armed Forces and Head of the Federal Military Government for the short period necessary to carry through the measures which are now urgently required.

In this period of emergency, no political statements in the Press, on the Radio and Television and all publicity media or any other political activity will be tolerated. The Military and Police are empowered to deal summarily with any offenders. Newspaper editors are particularly urged to co-operate with the authorities to ensure the success of these measures.

I have referred earlier to some illegal acts of the Eastern Region Government. You all know that about one-third of the entire rolling stock of the Nigerian Railways, including 115 oil-tankers, have been detained and that the services on the Eastern District of the Nigerian Railways have been competely disrupted for many months. You are also aware of the fact that they have disrupted the direct movement of oil products from the refinery near Port Harcourt to the Northern Region. They have hindered the transit of goods to neighbouring countries and have even seized goods belonging to foreign countries. These acts have flagrantly violated normal international practice and disturbed friendly relations with our neighbours. That refinery is owned jointly by the Federal Government and Regional Governments. Illegally, since last year, the Authorities at Enugu have interfered with the flight routes of the Nigerian Airways. Only recently they committed the barbaric crime of hi-jacking a plane bound for Lagos from Benin. They have placed a ban on the residence of non-Easterners in the Eastern Region - an action which is against the Constitution and the fundamental provisions of our laws. They have continuously on the Press and Radio incited the people of Eastern Region to hatred of other Nigerian peoples and they have indulged in the crudest abuse of members of the Supreme Military Council, especially myself.

Despite all these, I have spared no effort to conciliate the East in recognition of their understandable grievances and fears since the tragic incidents of 1966. To this end I agreed with my other colleagues on the Supreme Military Council to the promulgation of Decree No. 8 which completely decentralized the Government of this country and even went further than the Republican Constitution as it existed before 15th January,

(APPENDIX III: TEXT OF BROADCAST BY MAJOR-GENERAL YAKUBU GOWON)

1966. But what has been the response of the Eastern Region Government? Complete rejection of Decree No. 8 and insistence on its separate existence as a sovereign unit.

Only recently, a group of distinguished citizens formed themselves into the National Conciliation Committee. They submitted recommendations aimed at reducing tension. These included the reciprocal abrogation of economic measures taken by the Federal Military Government and the seizure of Federal Statutory Corporations and Federal revenue by the Eastern Government. These reciprocal actions were to be taken within one week, that is, by 25th May, 1967. It is on record that I accepted the recommendations and issued instructions effective from Tuesday, May 23. Indeed I now understand that certain vehicles of the Posts and Telegraphs Department which went to the East in resumption of services have been illegally detained in that Region. The response of the East has been completely negative and they have continued their propaganda and stage-managed demonstrations for "independence."

Fellow citizens, I recognize however that the problem of Nigeria extends beyond the present misguided actions of the Eastern Region Government. My duty is to all citizens. I propose to treat all sections of the country with equality. The main obstacle to future stability in this country is the present structural imbalance in the Nigerian Federation.

Even Decree No. 8 or Confederation or Loose Association will never survive if any one section of the country is in a position to hold the others to ransom.

This is why the item in the Political and Administrative Programme adopted by the Supreme Military Council last month is the creation of states as a basis for stability. This must be done first so as to remove the fear of domination. Representatives drawn from the new states will be more able to work out the future constitution for this country which can contain provisions to protect the powers of the states to the fullest extent desired by the Nigerian people. As soon as these states are established, a new Revenue Allocation Commission consisting of international experts will be appointed to recommend an equitable formula for revenue allocation taking into account the desires of the states.

I propose to act faithfully within the Political and Administrative Programme adopted by the Supreme Military Council and published last month. The world will recognize in these proposals our desire for justice and fair play for all sections of this country and to accommodate all genuine aspirations of the diverse people of this great country.

I have ordered the reimposition of the economic measures designed to safeguard Federal interests until such a time as the Eastern Military Government abrogates its

(APPENDIX III: TEXT OF BROADCAST BY MAJOR-GENERAL YAKUBU GOWON)

illegal edicts on revenue collection and the administration of the Federal Statutory
Corporations based in the East.

The country has a long history of well articulated demands for states. The fears
of minorities were explained in great detail and set out in the report of the Willink
Commission appointed by the British in 1958. More recently there has been extensive
discussions in Regional Consultative Committees and Leaders-of-Thought Conferences.
Resolutions have been adopted demanding the creation of states in the North and in
Lagos. Petititions from minority areas in the East which have been subjected to
violent intimidation by the Eastern Military Government have been widely publicized.
While the present circumstances regrettably do not allow for consultations through
plebiscites, I am satisfied that the creation of new states as the only possible basis
for stability and equality is the overwhelming desires of vast majority of Nigerians.
To ensure justice, these states are being created simultaneously.

To this end, therefore, I am promulgating a Decree which will divide the Federal
Republic into Twelve States. The twelve states will be six in the present Northern
Region, three in the present Eastern Region, the Mid-West will remain as it is, the
Colony Province of the Western Region and Lagos will form a new Lagos State and the
Western Region will otherwise remain as it is.

I must emphasize at once that the Decree will provide for a States Delimitation
Commission which will ensure that any divisions or towns not satisfied with the
states in which they are initially grouped will obtain redress. But in this moment of
serious National Emergency the co-operation of all concerned is absolutely essential
in order to avoid any unpleasant consequences.

I wish also to emphasize that an Administrative Council will be established at the
capitals of the existing regions which will be available to the new states to ensure the
smoothest possible administrative transition in the establishment of the new states.
The twelve new states, subject to marginal boundary adjustments, will therefore be
as follows:

North-Western State comprising Sokoto and Niger Provinces.
North-Central State comprising Katsina and Zaria.
Kano State comprising the present Kano Province.
North-Eastern State comprising Bornu, Adamawa, Sardauna and Bauchi Privinces.
Benue/Plateau State comprising Benue and Plateau Provinces.
West-Central State comprising Ilorin and Kabba Provinces.
Lagos State comprising the Colony Province and the Federal Territory of Lagos.
Western State comprising the present Western Region but excluding the Colony
Province.
Mid-Western State comprising the present Mid-Western State.

# Nigerian Civil War: An Annotated Bibliography

<u>East-Central State</u> comprising the present Eastern Region excluding Calabar, Ogoja and Rivers Provinces.
<u>South-Eastern State</u> comprising Calabar and Ogoja Provinces.
<u>Rivers State</u> comprising Ahoada, Brass, Degema, Ogoni and Port Harcourt Divisions.

The states will be free to adopt any particular names they choose in the future. The immediate administrative arrangements for the new states have been planned and the names of the Military Governors appointed to the new states will be gazetted shortly. The allocation of federally collected revenue to the new states on an interim basis for the first few months has also been planned. The successor states in each former region will share the revenue until a more permanent formula is recommended by the new Revenue Allocation Commission. Suitable arrangements have been made to minimize any disruption in the normal functioning of services in the areas of the new states.

It is my fervent hope that the existing Regional Authorities will co-operate fully to ensure the smoothest possible establishment of the new states. It is also my hope that the need to use force to support any new state will not arise. I am, however, ready to protect any citizens of this country who are subject to intimidation or violence in the course of establishment of these new states.

My dear countrymen, the struggle ahead is for the well-being of the present and future generations of Nigerians. If it were possible for us to avoid chaos and civil war merely by drifting apart as some people claim, that easy choice may have been taken. But we know that to take such a course will quickly lead to the disintegration of the existing regions in condition of chaos and to disastrous foreign interference. We now have to adopt the courageous course of facing the fundamental problem that has plagued this country since the early 50's. There should be no recrimination. We must all resolve to work together. It is my hope that those who disagreed in the past with the Federal Military Government through genuine misunderstanding and mistrust will now be convinced of our purpose and be willing to come back and let us plan and work together for the realization of the Political and Administrative programme of the Supreme Military Council, and for the early restoration of full civilian rule in circumstances which would enhance just and honest and patriotic government. I appeal to the general public to continue to give their co-operation to the Federal Military Government; to go about their normal business peacefully; to maintain harmony with all communities wherever they live; to respect all the directives of the Government including directives restricting the movements of people while the emergency remains. Such directives are for their own protection and in their own interest.

Let us, therefore, march manfully together to alter the course of this nation once

(APPENDIX III:  TEXT OF BROADCAST BY MAJOR–GENERAL YAKUBU GOWON)

and for all and to place it on the path of progress, unity and equality.  Let us so act that future generations of Nigerians will praise us for our resolution and courage in this critical stage of our country's history.  Long live the Federal Republic of Nigeria!

APPENDIX IV: MAJOR RELIEF AGENCIES

## Major Relief Agencies

1. ABC (Aid to Biafran Children) organized by <u>Saturday Review</u>, an American magazine.

2. The American Committee to Keep Biafra Alive, (joining other international humanitarian agencies after the war to form International Conscience In Action).

3. The American Jewish Emergency Effort for Biafran Relief.

4. The American Red Cross.

5. Australian Catholic Relief.

6. BROTHER (Biafra Rescue Organization to Hasten Emergency Relief) (U.S.A.).

7. Biafra Relief Services Foundation (U.S.A.).

8. The Biafra Union (Britain).

9. Bishops Emergency Relief Committee (U.S.A.).

10. The Britain-Biafra Association.

11. The British Red Cross.

12. The Canadian Red Cross.

13. Canairelief (Canada).

14. Caritas Internationalis (The Vatican, Italy).

15. Catholic Relief Services, (bringing relief to 72 countries). (U.S.A.)

16. Church World Service, (representing 30 U.S. Protestant denominations and bringing relief to 42 countries).

17. The CORSO, (New Zealand).

18. Diakonische Werk (Germany).

19. Food for Biafra Committee (U.S.A.).

*Nigerian Civil War: An Annotated Bibliography*

(APPENDIX IV:  MAJOR RELIEF AGENCIES)


20.  The France-Biafra Association.

21.  The France-Nigeria Association.

22.  The French Committee for Action on Biafra.

23.  The French Red Cross.

24.  The Friends of Biafra Association  (Britain).

25.  The International Committee of the Red Cross.

26.  Joint Church Aid (representing 33 Catholic, Protestant and Jewish organizations from 21 countries).

27.  Medical Support Program for Biafra-Nigeria  (U.S.A.).

28.  National  Council of Catholic Women  (U.S.A.).

29.  The Nigerian Committee of California  (U.S.A.).

30.  OXFAM  (Britain).

31.  The Save Biafra Campaign  (Britain).

32.  Susan Garth Babies Appeal  (Britain).

33.  The Swedish Red Cross.

34.  The Swiss Red Cross.

35.  Terre des Hommes  (Canada).

36.  UNICEF  (United Nations Children's Emergency Fund).

37.  Unitarian Universalist Service Committee  (U.S.A.).

38.  The World Council of Churches.

APPENDIX V: TEXT OF THE BIAFRAN SURRENDER

Text of the Biafran Surrender

Before handing over the surrender document to Nigerian leader Major-General Gowon on January 15, 1970, Biafran Army Chief of Staff, Philip Effiong, read its contents aloud, as follows:

I, Philip Effiong, do hereby declare:

I give you not only my own personal assurances but also those of my fellow officers and colleagues and of the entire former Biafran people of our fullest co-operation and very sincere best wishes for the future.

It is my sincere hope that the lessons of the bitter struggle have been well learned by everybody, and I would like therefore to take this opportunity to say that I, Major-General Philip Effiong, Officer Administering the Government of the Republic of Biafra, now wish to make the following declaration:

That we are loyal Nigerian citizens and accept the authority of the Federal Military Government of Nigeria.

That we accept the existing administrative and political structure of the Federation of Nigeria.

That any future Constitutional arrangement will be worked out by representatives of the people of Nigeria.

That the Republic of Biafra hereby ceases to exist.

APPENDIX VI: NATIONAL ANTHEM

<u>National Anthem</u>

Nigeria we hail thee,
Our own dear native land,
Though tribe and tongue may differ,
In brotherhood we stand,
Nigerians all, and proud to serve
Our sovereign Mother land.

Our flag shall be a symbol
That truth and justice reign,
In peace or battle honour'd
And this we count as gain,
To hand on to our children,
A banner without stain.

O God of all Creation,
Grant this our one request,
Help us to build a nation
Where no man is oppressed,
And so with peace and plenty
Nigeria may be blessed.

## AUTHOR INDEX

(AUTHOR INDEX)

(AUTHOR INDEX)

(AUTHOR INDEX)